THE PRINCE,
THE SHOWGIRL AND ME

THE PRINCE, THE SHOWGIRL AND ME

The Colin Clark Diaries

HarperCollins*Publishers*

HarperCollins*Publishers*
77–85 Fulham Palace Road,
Hammersmith, London W6 8JB
Published by HarperCollins*Publishers* 1995

A catalogue record for this book is
available from the British Library

ISBN 0 00 255642 1

Photoset in Linotron Fournier by
Rowland Phototypesetting Ltd,
Bury St Edmunds, Suffolk.

Printed in Great Britain by
HarperCollinsManufacturing Glasgow

For Christopher and Helena,
with love

Contents

ILLUSTRATIONS

Marilyn Monroe and Arthur Miller arrive at Heathrow, escorted by my friends, the policemen. (*Press Association*)

Laurence Olivier and Vivien Leigh greet MM and AM at the airport. (*Hulton Deutsch*)

Crowds of reporters force MM and SLO to take refuge behind a counter at Heathrow. (*Syndication International*)

MM with Donald Zec of the *Mirror*, shortly after arriving at Parkside House. Zec had just jumped out of the bushes, and MM had no idea who he was. (*Syndication International*)

AM, MM and SLO on arrival at Parkside House. My head can just be seen through the window. (*Popperfoto*)

Vivien Leigh and SLO in *The Sleeping Prince*, Phoenix Theatre, 1953. (*Popperfoto*)

Roger Furse's original design for the salon, much changed for the actual filming. (*British Film Institute*)

MM at the start of filming. (*British Film Institute*)

Richard Wattis, Andrea Melandrinos, SLO, Jack Cardiff and Denys Coop. (*British Film Institute*)

Elaine Schreyck, Terence Rattigan, an exasperated SLO, an electrician and Tony Bushell on the 'purple room' set. (*British Film Institute*)

Dame Sybil Thorndike, MM, Richard Wattis. MM loved Dame Sybil, but still couldn't remember her lines. (*Syndication International*)

Vivien Leigh overcome by Carpathian vodka and champagne in *The Sleeping Prince*. (*Popperfoto*)

MM about to be overcome in *The Prince and the Showgirl*. (*The Kobal Collection*)

The young King (Jeremy Spenser) watches Elsie Marina doing her very charming dance routine in the purple sitting room. (*Aquarius Library*)

MM and SLO surrounded by dancing club extras in the ballroom scene. MM genuinely loved to dance. (*British Film Institute*)

The coach about to jolt into motion. All but Dame Sybil are already tensed in anticipation. (*The Kobal Collection*)

Production unit photograph of *The Prince and the Showgirl*. (*British Film Institute*)

MM, standing between Victor Mature and Anthony Quayle, meets the Queen at the Royal Film Premiere of *The Battle of the River Plate*. MM and HM were almost exactly the same age. (*Popperfoto*)

PREFACE

In 1943, when I was ten years old, my boarding school decided that my class should see *Gone with the Wind*. Film shows were a monthly treat then, and we had already seen several stirring black-and-white wartime epics, but *Gone with the Wind* was different. It was in colour, it was very long, and it contained some gruesome scenes of wounded soldiers, the sort of thing which was obviously never included in British films of the time. Our teacher took great trouble to explain to us that the film was just an illusion, made up of clever special effects. Nevertheless, watching it in that bare school hall had a dramatic effect on all of us.

At about the same time my father, Kenneth Clark, had been made controller of home publicity at the Ministry of Information. This meant that he was responsible for extricating British actors and actresses from the armed forces so that they could work in patriotic films. He made frequent visits to the studios around London to see how they were getting on, and I persuaded him to let me come too. His principal ally was Alexander Korda, who was the most powerful British producer at the time, and whom my father had persuaded to join in the 'war effort'. Through him my father and mother met all the stars of the film world. Laurence Olivier and Vivien Leigh became their close friends, and William Walton, who was composing the music for Olivier's *Henry V*, was made my godfather to replace the original one who had been killed by a bomb. Another Hungarian producer, Gabriel Pascal, had managed to persuade George Bernard Shaw to let him have the

film rights to all his plays. He came to our house in Hampstead
with a beautiful young American actress called Irene Worth,
and promised to buy me a pair of white peacocks if I would
act for him, offering me the part of Ptolemy in his production
of Shaw's *Caesar and Cleopatra* (with Vivien Leigh). My parents
said no, but I was not the least bit disappointed: I knew that I
could never be an actor, and I also knew that those white
peacocks were as much a product of Pascal's imagination as
Caesar and Cleopatra was of Shaw's.

I had become completely fascinated by the concept of a fic-
tional idea being made into a real film, which is in itself an
illusion. It is a fascination which I have never lost. At the age
of twelve I explained this to my father, and told him of my
determination to be a film director. My only worry was that all
the directors I had met were fat and ugly. To my surprise he
took me seriously. Although he was involved in all the performing arts – opera, ballet and theatre as well as film – his
main love was painting. He pointed out that painting contains
the same elements of illusion and reality as film, and that
Michael Powell and David Lean were both successful directors,
and they were thin.

From then on, a visit to a film set was like a dream fulfilled.
I saw Noël Coward in a tank of oily black water making *In
Which We Serve*; I saw Vivien Leigh being carried on a very
wobbly litter in front of a plaster Sphinx on the set of *Caesar
and Cleopatra*; I saw her again in *Anna Karenina* – she had offered
me the role of her son, again refused; and many more. I was
not in love with the magic of film the way many children are
with theatre or ballet: I was in love with the way in which that
magic was made.

When I got to Eton in 1946 it became clear that I had chosen
a pretty eccentric path. 'Art' did not then have the respectable
connotations that it does today. My family, though wealthy
enough, was as far from the typical 'hunting, shooting and

fishing' set as it was possible to be. None of my more conventional contemporaries had ever heard of an art historian, and I was forced to describe my father as a professor (he had been Slade Professor of Fine Art at Oxford). My friends could not understand me at all – many still can't – and as if to underline the difference between us, I chose to be a pilot in the RAF during my National Service rather than to go into the Guards, and then to get a job as a keeper at London Zoo rather than work in a merchant bank.

In the summer of 1952, while on vacation from Oxford, I went on a motoring tour of Europe and found myself stranded in a little palace in the mountains of north Portugal. It belonged to an Englishman called Peter Pitt-Millward, and apart from his occasional guests, I had no one else with whom to converse for over two months. To make things worse, I fell passionately in love with someone who could speak nothing but Portuguese. I could not even confide in Peter about this as he was also in love – with the same person. So I started to keep a daily journal in which I could explore my emotions, and my loneliness. This feeling of isolation persisted throughout the remainder of my time at university.

By the time I got the job on *The Prince and the Showgirl* in 1956, my diary had become a firm friend. However tired I was, I could not sleep before I had written down some of the things that had happened during the day, and confided some of the opinions that I had not dared to express to anyone, scribbling away in an old ledger which I kept wrapped up in my pyjamas. I did not always get things right, and as I never expected anyone else to read what I had written, I had no need to be what we now call 'politically correct'. Even so, in this published version of my diary for June to November 1956, I have cut very little out. I was a well-brought-up boy, and when you see 'f—' in this book it is because I wrote 'f—' in my diary.

When the filming of *The Prince and the Showgirl* was over, it was many, many years before I dared to read my diary of that time again, just as it was many, many years before I could bring myself to see the film in a cinema. Even now I have trouble seeing past the pain and anxiety in Marilyn Monroe's eyes.

This book is really all about Marilyn. For five months, whether she turned up or not, she dominated our every waking thought. I was the least important person in the whole studio, but I was in a wonderful position from which to observe. The Third Assistant Director is really a kind of superior messenger boy. I got to meet everyone and go everywhere, unencumbered by responsibilities which might tie me down, or narrow my viewpoint. No one can feel threatened by a 3rd Ast Dir (except perhaps the 'extras', who he has to keep under control), and most of the people involved in making the film felt they could be more open with me than with a possible rival. When the filming was completed I was almost the only person who was still on speaking terms with everyone else. That alone probably makes this diary unique.

The Prince and the Showgirl
Cast List

ELSIE MARINA	*Marilyn Monroe*
THE REGENT OF CARPATHIA	*Laurence Olivier*
THE QUEEN DOWAGER	*Sybil Thorndike*
MR NORTHBROOK	*Richard Wattis*
THE KING OF CARPATHIA	*Jeremy Spenser*
MAJOR DOMO	*Paul Hardwick*
MAISIE SPRINGFIELD	*Jean Kent*
LADY SUNNINGDALE	*Maxine Audley*
FANNY	*Daphne Anderson*
BETTY	*Vera Day*
MAGGIE	*Gillian Owen*
FOREIGN OFFICE MINISTER	*David Horne*
THEATRE DRESSER	*Gladys Henson*
HOFFMAN	*Esmond Knight*
LADIES-IN-WAITING	*Rosamund Greenwood* *Margot Lister*
VALETS	*Dennis Edwards* *Andrea Melandrinos*

Production Crew

PRODUCER AND DIRECTOR	*Laurence Olivier*
EXECUTIVE IN CHARGE OF PRODUCTION	*Hugh Perceval*
EXECUTIVE PRODUCER	*Milton Greene*
ASSOCIATE DIRECTOR	*Anthony Bushell*
FIRST ASSISTANT DIRECTOR	*David Orton*
DIRECTOR OF PHOTOGRAPHY	*Jack Cardiff*
PRODUCTION DESIGNER	*Roger Furse*
PRODUCTION MANAGER	*Teddy Joseph*
ART DIRECTION	*Carmen Dillon*
EDITOR	*Jack Harris*
CONTINUITY	*Elaine Schreyck*
CAMERA OPERATOR	*Denys Coop*
SOUND RECORDISTS	*John Mitchell* *Gordon McCallum*
LADIES' COSTUMES	*Beatrice Dawson*
MAKE-UP	*Toni Sforzini*
HAIRDRESSING	*Gordon Bond*
SET DRESSER	*Dario Simoni*
SCREENPLAY	*Terence Rattigan*
MUSIC COMPOSED BY	*Richard Addinsell*
DANCES ARRANGED BY	*William Chappell*

THE DIARIES

SUNDAY, 3 JUNE 1956

Now that University is behind me, I'm going to get a job – a real job on a real film. At 9 a.m. tomorrow I will be at Laurence Olivier's film company to offer my services on his next production. The papers say it will star Marilyn Monroe, so it should be exciting.

Two weeks ago, Larry and Vivien came down to stay at Saltwood* for the weekend. Mama told Vivien that I wanted to be a film director. I was mortified, but Vivien just gave a great purr and said 'Larry will give Colin a job, won't you Larry darling!' I could see Larry groan under his breath. 'Go and see Hugh Perceval at 146 Piccadilly,' he said. 'He might have something.'

So that is where I have an appointment in the morning. And every night I am going to write this diary. It could be fun to look back on, when I am old and famous!

MONDAY, 4 JUNE

This is going to be really hard. I know absolutely nothing about making films. I'm totally ignorant. Did I really think they were actually shooting a film in Piccadilly?

At 10 a.m. I turned up at the office of Laurence Olivier Productions, punctual and sober.

The offices themselves are very few. A large luxurious reception area with sofas, a secretary's office at the far end, and Mr Perceval's office leading off that. It is clearly the ground

* Saltwood Castle in Kent, my parents' home.

floor of what was once a private house. The secretary, friendly but detached – would I wait. Mr Perceval was on the phone. Soon I was ushered in, anxious now. There didn't seem to be enough going on. Mr P is a tall, thin, gloomy man with black-rim spectacles. His sparse black hair is brushed back and he has a black moustache. He puffs a pipe continually.

'Yes. What do you want?' (No introductions whatever.)

'I want a job on the Marilyn Monroe film.'

'Oh, ho, you do? What as?'

'Anything.'

I suppose he could see that I was a complete fool and he softened a little.

'Well. We don't start filming for eight weeks. You really should come back then. At the moment we have no more offices than you can see here, and no jobs. I only have my chauffeur and my secretary. I am afraid I misunderstood Laurence. I thought you were coming to interview me about the film.'

Blind panic set in. I must say something.

'Can I wait here until there is a job?'

'For eight weeks??'

'In the waiting room – in case something comes up?'

'Grmph.' Very gloomy, and bored now. 'It's a free country, I suppose. But I'm telling you, it's going to be eight weeks. And then I can't promise anything.'

Gets up and opens door.

'Good day.'

I went out and sat down on one of the sofas in the waiting room. The secretary gave me a very cold look. She's quite pretty, but is certainly not flirtatious.

I just didn't know what to do. I had expected huge offices, even studios, lots of work going on – willing hands needed in every department, and a bit like the London Zoo when I turned

up there and asked for a job as a keeper in '53 (and got one!*).
So I just sat and waited.

At lunchtime I was saved by a friendly face. Gilman, Larry
and Vivien's chauffeur came in, brash and cockney as ever.

''Ullo Colin. What you doin' 'ere?'

I explained.

'Hmm. There's no work here. I've got to get his nibs' lunch.
Come and have a drink in the pub.'

I went gratefully (but only ½ of bitter). Gilman told me what
was going on. He was on loan to Perceval. Every morning he
did errands, for Perceval or for Larry, and then came back here
to get Perceval's lunch. This never varied: two cheese rolls and
a Guinness.

'You won't get work from him, Colin. Miserable bugger.'

'Well, I've got nothing else in the world to do but wait, so
I might as well wait.'

'OK. Good luck. We can always have a pint together at
lunchtime.'

We went back with Mr P's sandwiches and drink and Gilman
sped off in the Bentley. I waited until 6 p.m., when they all
packed up and left.

'Night all,' said Mr P gloomily, without a glance at me. I had
a large brandy and water in the pub. I'll be back in the office
tomorrow.

TUESDAY, 5 JUNE

I was there at 8.30. The secretary arrived at 8.55. Mr P punctu-
ally at nine. He just gave me a grim stare as he came in. Then
he gets on the phone and stays there most of the day. He never
smiles and he never raises his voice. The secretary gets the
calls for him and then taps away at the typewriter. She is polite

* In the tropical bird house.

but not friendly. She treats me like a client. I wonder if she knows that 'M and D'* are friends of Larry and Vivien?

She went to lunch at 12.30 with her handbag and gloves. Gilman arrived at 12.45. Then we went to the pub, and got back with Mr P's lunch at 1.15. I wonder if this is a regular situation. Maybe I can make something out of it. Mr P grumbles at the delay but Gilman is irrepressible.

Vivien had told me why she had hired Gilman. He was a relief driver, sent along when their old chauffeur was ill. On the first day, as he drove her and Larry down Bond Street, he suddenly slammed on the brakes. 'Cor. Look, what a lovely waistcoat!' he cried, pointing to a very exclusive man's-shop window. Vivien adores that sort of unspoilt character and hired him on the spot. Needless to say he now worships both of them, and is fanatically loyal. He is a Barnardo boy and very tough, so Larry probably thinks he is a good bodyguard for Vivien too. He certainly is a good pal to me and saves my life when he appears.

I get a bit nervous in my role as the invisible man. But I was more relaxed there today, and so was the secretary.

Now I've got to use my head.

WEDNESDAY, 6 JUNE

Yes. There is a pattern, and it should be possible to exploit it.

I am completely ignored all morning, but as there is no door between the waiting room and the secretary's office, I hear quite a lot. Also, she often leaves Mr P's door open when she is in there with him.

Today I didn't go to the pub with Gillers. I just gave him a wink which he picked up immediately. This meant Mr P was

* My shorthand way of describing my parents. Five years previously they had told me to stop calling them 'Mum and Dad' and to address them as 'Mama and Papa'.

alone for 45 minutes. During this time, he keeps on working and the phones keep ringing.

He has three lines. I just ignored them, but after five minutes he opened his door and glared at the empty secretary's desk. Then he slammed his door shut again. Two minutes of phone ringing later, he opened it again and glared some more, this time at me.

'You still here? Well you might as well answer the phone. Don't think you've got a job, though. There's no chance of that at all.'

He slammed out.

Phone rings. Mr P answers. Next phone rings.

'Hello. Is that Laurence Olivier Productions?'

'Yes. Can I help you.'

'Is Sir Laurence there?'

'No, I'm afraid he's in America until the end of the week.'

'Oh. Thank you. I'll ring next week.'

'Any message?'

'No thank you.'

Click. Mr P's door opens.

'How did you know that Sir Laurence is in America until the end of the week?'

'I heard him tell my mother.'

'Hmph. Why didn't you put the call through to me?' (There is a buzzer on each phone.)

'There didn't seem to be a need to bother you. But if you want every single call . . .'

'Hmph.'

Door slams again. Phone rings.

'Laurence Olivier Productions.' I'm chirpy now!

'Is Mr Perceval there?'

'Certainly. Whom shall I say is calling?'

'The *Daily Mirror*.'

'Hold on please.' Click. Bzzz. 'Yes?'

'The *Daily Mirror* for you.'

'Hmph.'

I put through about eight calls, and I was beginning to enjoy it when the secretary (Vanessa) came back at 1.30. She didn't look very happy at first, but I had left her a note of all calls and messages, so she began to smile again.

Finally Gillers returned with Mr P's rolls and Guinness. He was 20 minutes late and he gave me another terrific wink, which I was frightened that Mr P saw, but he gave no sign.

I had hoped to go back to the pub for my lunch with Gillers, but Mr P sent him straight down to Notley.* So I had to go alone. I had a large pink gin with my sandwich, and sure enough no one addressed a word to me all afternoon.

But it doesn't matter. At least I have a role to play from 12.30 to 1.30. I must make the most of it.

FRIDAY, 8 JUNE

By now Mr P takes it for granted that I am on duty at lunchtime. Only one week here and already I am part of the furniture.

Being efficient is the easy part. Suppressing one's ego completely for hours at a time is really hard. Gilman phoned in to say he was staying with Vivien all day, and what Vivien wants, Vivien gets; no question of that.

I went round to the pub and got two cheese rolls and a Guinness *before* Vanessa left at 12.30. Then at 12.45 I walked silently into Mr P's office and put it on his desk. Mr P was on the phone – a long-distance call to America (he must have got someone out of bed). He puffed at his pipe and gave me a mournful stare over the top of his hornrim glasses. I think he realises I'm going to win in the end! I crept out and shut the door without a word from either of us.

* Notley Abbey, Laurence Olivier and Vivien Leigh's home in Buckinghamshire.

24

When Vanessa came back, I left. 'See you Monday,' I said. '8.30 sharp.' She just laughed, but in a friendly way. I'll bet she reports every word I say to Mr P. At the same time, her private life is obviously more important to her than her job – unlike Mr P, or me for that matter. So she is really a non-combatant.

After lunch I got in the car and came down here to Saltwood for a break.

'How is the new job?' asked Mama.

'Very good.'

'Settling in nicely? It was kind of Larry to give it to you.'

But she is too shrewd to be convinced. Actually I don't think she believes either of her sons can get a good job or ever will.

I told Celly* the minimum. She is incredibly sympathetic as usual, but she leads such a busy life that I didn't think I could quite explain my 'wait eight weeks' policy. It does sound a bit hopeless when looked at from down here, but I am committed to it.

MONDAY, 11 JUNE

I was surprised to find myself glad to be back at 146 Piccadilly at 8.30 this morning.

Vanessa turned up at 8.55 with another girl. Are there to be two secretaries from now on? Mr P has moved faster than I thought, hence the mournful stare. My heart went to my boots, but incredibly, at 12.30 they both went out together for lunch. By this time I had already rushed out to the pub and got Mr P's two cheese rolls and Guinness. If Gilman had turned up I would have explained, but luckily he didn't, so I was alone as usual. Vanessa and her companion regard me with complete indifference and don't seem to be bothered by Mr P either. They chattered away all morning as if he hardly mattered,

* My twin sister Colette.

except for phone calls and typing. I think he is scared of them.
When I took his lunch in at 12.45 he didn't even look up. 'War
of nerves'. However, by 1 p.m. he needed help.

'I need to find the telephone number of someone called Noël
Coward.'

He pronounced the name very carefully as if I was an idiot.

'It won't be in the telephone book. You will have to call X,
and he will know the number of Y, and Y should know Mr
Coward's number. He will give it to you if you say you are
calling for me.'

'Yes, Mr Perceval.'

I rang Saltwood.

'Oh Col, how lovely to hear you.' (I had only been gone 14
hours.)

'Mama, this is urgent. I need Noël Coward's phone number
in England, right away.'

'How exciting.' I could hear Mama looking at her voluminous
card index. 'Here it is.'

Straight into Mr P's office with the number on a piece of
paper. No time to check it. I put it on his desk: NOËL COWARD
and the number.

'Hmph.' Dark look. 'That was very quick.' Grudgingly: 'Good.'

Ah, these tiny triumphs! And it must have been the right
number or he would certainly have complained.

I stayed late to savour my success and try to glean something
from the girls' gossip. Absolutely nothing.

But Mr P said 'Goodnight Colin' as he went out.

TUESDAY, 12 JUNE

At 11 o'clock, a boring morning was interrupted by much
kerfuffle outside.

Then in strode Larry. He was taken aback to see me (probably couldn't recognise me at first) but managed 'Hello, dear

boy' before disappearing into Mr P's office. I expect his first question was 'Who the hell's that?' and the second 'What the hell's he doing here?'

A few seconds later in comes Vivien, followed by a grinning Gilman. (He will have briefed her after Larry left the car. Vivien is *never* caught off guard!)

'Colin, darling.'

Vivien comes up so close to me that our noses are almost touching. She gives a pleading look: 'Please look after my darling Larry for me, will you?'

She flutters her eyelids, gives a small quick confidential smile and sweeps off into Mr P's office, ignoring the two girls. I am left standing in the middle of the reception room, as if struck by lightning. Vivien does pack about 100,000 volts, and she completely stuns me. The two secretaries are equally dumbfounded.

After 10 minutes, Vivien reappears, kisses me on both cheeks, with her lips pointing at my ears, and goes off with Gilman. Larry stays about an hour. As he goes out he says: 'Do find this dear boy something to do, Hughie.'

Then a very charming and sincere goodbye to each secretary before he and Mr P go off for lunch at the Ivy.

After five minutes, the girls had recovered their composure and went out to lunch, again together, leaving me to answer the phones and take messages. They now regard me as a convenient fixture, but I wonder what they would have done if I didn't exist. The same I expect.

When Mr P comes back he says: 'I might have a job for you tomorrow, Colin. (Colin!!) Just one day's work, mind. Nothing permanent, you hear. No chance of that. So be in early in the morning.'

Hasn't he noticed that I am always here first? Maybe it's part of his 'Keep Colin in his place' strategy. Anyway I've refused a really good party tonight. I hope my virtue is rewarded.

WEDNESDAY, 13 JUNE

Work at last.

I arrived at 8.30 and Mr P came in almost immediately. Vanessa too. (She must have been warned!)

'Come straight in, Colin.'

Mr P had a problem.

MM's publicity man is coming to London tomorrow. He wants to see the house MM is going to stay in while she is in England for the filming. Mr P hates publicity men and thinks this one is fussing much too early. Naturally no one has started to look at houses yet.

Mr P wants me to find a suitable house today. It must be no more than 40 minutes' drive from Pinewood Studios and no more than 40 minutes' drive from central London. Minimum three double bedrooms and three bathrooms plus ample servants' quarters. It must be surrounded by gardens and well off a main road. It must be ultra-luxurious. Price no object.

'Check the estate agents. You can have one of these phone lines all morning. Report back to me by 5 p.m. I'm putting my trust in you. Don't let me down.'

My mind was racing. I walked out of the offices and went and sat in the car. 40 minutes was about 20 miles. I didn't even know where Pinewood Studios were. I got out the AA map, found Pinewood and made a rough 20-mile arc around it. Ah-hah. Ascot. I walked down Piccadilly to the St James's Club.

'Morning Mr Colin.'

'Morning Lockhart. Mr Cotes-Preedy in yet?'

'Not yet, but he's always in by noon.'

'Good.'

Enough time for a hearty breakfast. Last year Tim R* and I

* Tim Rathbone, with whom I had been at Eton and Oxford. Elected Conservative MP for Lewes in 1974.

had rented a tiny cottage from Mr Cotes-Preedy's wife. They lived in the big house, Tibbs Farm, opposite Ascot Racecourse. It was up a long drive and was exactly what Mr P had specified. Mrs C-P is a splendid lady – much older than her husband and looking like a macaw, but somehow attractive and even sexy. They were both very fond of money, like all the Ascot crowd.

After breakfast, I still had a long wait, and I made a lot more phone calls. I'm going to try to pull off a stunt. If I don't do something to surprise Mr P I'll be sitting in that waiting room forever.

By the time Mr C-P arrived I was all fired up. Mr C-P is a lawyer. He was surprised to see me but he did remember me – he's seen me occasionally in the bar. I put the proposition to him in stages.

'Rent the main house? Out of the question. Mrs C-P would never agree ... £100 per week!!! For 18 weeks? Famous film star?' He simply shot to the phone to call Mrs C-P and came back all smiles.

Copious drinks bought for everyone in the bar. (Only one for me.) Some more frantic phone calls, lunch, and back to Mr P by 3 p.m.

Raised eyebrows. 'Hmph. Hmph. Hmph.' But he didn't dare call my bluff.

'Have you got a car?'

'Yes.'

'You are to be at the Savoy Hotel at 9 a.m. tomorrow and ask for Mr Arthur P. Jacobs.* He's MM's publicity man and he has to approve the house. Take him to see it in your car and then bring him back here to me.'

I left and came straight home. I rang Mr C-P to confirm that Mrs C-P would be ready for us, and then washed the car, inside and out.

* Arthur P. Jacobs (1918–73) later became a producer. His films included *Dr Dolittle* (1967) and *Planet of the Apes* (1968).

Now I can't sleep because of my gamble, but, to be honest, I haven't that much to lose. Just an awful lot to gain.

THURSDAY, 14 JUNE

I got to the Savoy at 8.45 a.m. At nine I went in and told the concierge. He looked up Jacobs and said he had a wake-up call booked for 10 a.m. (!) so I went back and sat in the car until eleven, then checked again. 'Yes, he had been called at 10 a.m.,' and 'Don't bother me again, you serf,' implied.

At 11.30, APJ emerged. Close-cropped black hair, pugnacious, bad tempered, puffy face. Naturally no apology – not even good morning or hello. He looked at my car with great disgust and got in.

He was carrying one copy of every single newspaper you can buy, and these he proceeded to read until we were on the A4 by the airport. Then quite suddenly he wound down his window and threw the whole lot out. I could see them in my mirror, blowing all over the road, blinding other drivers. It seemed to me the single most anti-social act I had ever seen. I couldn't resist a protest.

'In England we do not normally behave like that,' I said icily.

'Whadja talking about?'

'Throwing all those newspapers out of the window. They caused a terrible mess.'

'I'd finished with them.'

Nothing more to say.

I can't believe everyone does that in America. He's just a totally egocentric and insensitive boor, and that's that.

But I soon had my revenge. The passenger seat back on the Bristol rests on two chrome 'cams'. If I corner too fast to the left it slips off these cams, and falls back flat. The first corner I came to off the A4 was a left-hander. I was grinding my teeth with rage and consequently driving faster than normal. Suffice it to say that for a fraction of a second Mr Jacobs thought that he was falling through the bottom of the car onto the road. Of course I stopped and helped him to sit up again, with many sincere apologies. But he looked pale, and at last he actually noticed who I was for a fleeting moment.

We were very late for Mrs C-P at Tibbs, but the house is exactly as I remembered it. Thick gold Wilton, heavy curtains, eau-de-nil bathrooms etc. surrounded by dark foliage. Mrs C-P all charm and very excited: 'Your friends were here,' she said to me but APJ, unremittingly odious, took no notice.

After 20 minutes we drove back to Piccadilly. No lunch of course. I suppose APJ had had a healthy breakfast at the Savoy, but I'd had nothing since seven and I was in a bad temper.

'Well?' said Mr P, after giving APJ a patently false show of comradeship.

'Not bad, I suppose,' said APJ – just as I thought he would – and shut Mr P's office door in my face. I went out for lunch and made another phone call.

At 5 p.m. I wandered back in. It was now or never. Luckily it was now.

Mr P's office door was open. 'They want to see you right away,' said Vanessa. 'I'm afraid they're rather angry.'

'Good,' I said and marched in. APJ was in a corner, his face black with rage. 'Colin,' said Mr P, very growly, 'Have you seen this?' He held out the *Evening Standard*.

Headline: 'This is the house Marilyn Monroe will live in while in England blah blah.' Picture of Tibbs Farm.

'Yes, I have.'

'There is only one person who could have given the papers this story.'

'You must have given it to them before I even saw the house,' said APJ through clenched teeth.

'Of course I gave it to them.'

'Well now you've ruined everything. It was the perfect house, but once the press know of it, it is out of the question. Couldn't you have realised it had to stay a secret?'

'It wasn't the perfect house this morning.'

Mr P: 'Colin. What's going on?' He is a shrewd old bean. He knows that I like and admire him. He can't stand APJ and can see that I can't stand him either. Suddenly I saw it cross his mind, 'Maybe I can trust Colin after all.'

'When you told me to get a house for MM yesterday, I took the precaution of finding two. I showed Mr Jacobs the least good first. Now the press will always think that MM is staying there and we can rent the second house for her to live in. The second house is much better. It belongs to a Lord. I can take Mr Jacobs to see it now, or tomorrow morning, if he'd like. It is only a couple of miles from the first house, but it is much more elegant.'

Mr P: 'And what are we going to say to the owners of the first house?'

'I thought perhaps the production team could use it.'

'What do you know about production teams?'

Before I could admit to total ignorance, APJ suddenly recovered his composure. 'Hey, Milton and Amy could use it. It would be perfect. Near the studio, near Marilyn.' Now he was the PR man, selling it to us. I suppose that in Hollywood people like him have to jump backward somersaults every day.

Mr P: 'OK, that's settled then. Arrange for both houses to be rented from 9 July, for four months. By the way, how much are they?'

'£100 per week, each.'

Mr P's eyebrows went up. Then he brightened. 'Well, it comes out of Marilyn Monroe Productions' budget.'

'Don't you want to see the other house?' (I was really proud of it.)

'Nah, no need, we trust you boy.' Arthur had completely changed sides, and probably did not fancy another trip in the

Bristol. Mr P nodded towards the door, and I left. Soon APJ left too. 'See you, kid,' to me. 'Bye, sweetheart,' to the secretaries. Then Mr P: 'See you tomorrow, Colin.' Just a hint of a smile.

I call that victory.

FRIDAY, 15 JUNE

And a victory it is.

On Monday I start working on the staff of LOP Ltd, at £8.10s. per week, as Mr P's assistant. When I came in this morning, Mr P called me into his office and actually gave a grin. Somehow Arthur Jacobs had persuaded himself that the whole house business was *his* triumph and had gone away (to Paris) happy. Mr P loathes him – quite rightly, he's a bullying shit – and sees it as *his* success, a problem neatly solved by a member of his staff (!).

'Never trust that Hollywood crowd, Colin. The better you are, the more likely they are to stab you in the back.'

The secretaries already knew of my appointment and offered friendly congratulations. I've been living in their office for two weeks only now am I officially one of them. It means that I can share the gossip with Vanessa, which will be useful as well as fun.

Gilman bounded in and gave a whoop of delight. 'You can get his lunch now – official!'

It did seem rather wasteful for Sir Laurence and Lady Olivier's Bentley and chauffeur to be sent in every day just to get Mr P a cheese roll. The pub is only 100 yards away, but that's showbiz.

It seems that as from Monday there will be another LOP production office at Pinewood. They will have the job of hiring all the personnel and facilities needed to make the film, and the Pinewood accounts office will pay people too – including me.

Mr P promised to take me down to look over the studios in a few weeks' time.

'We'd better try to get you a job on the production side for later on. You won't want to stay with me once filming starts.'

He has become quite fatherly. I rang Cotes-Preedy who is very excited. Naturally he believes the newspaper report that MM is going to stay in his house, and I did not disabuse him. Then I rang Garrett Moore,* who owns house No 2. A bit of panic when he said the whole thing was off, but I guessed the problem. '£100 a week is not enough,' he said severely. He is extremely astute and can somehow tell he has me over a barrel. I had told him, on pain of death to keep it a secret, that MM was going to be the tenant, and since he fancies himself as God's gift to women, I knew he was not going to refuse. I'll bet he secretly thinks that he will get to meet her and that she will be unable to resist his languid charm. Eventually we settled for £120 per week. Mr P had said 'Price no object', so I didn't bother to check back with him. But I did insist on going down to Parkside House over the weekend. I just can't resist meeting Garrett's wife, Joan.** She is incredibly beautiful. I hope the house is also as attractive as I remember it. Right now I'm going out to get sloshed at the Stork.*** To eat, drink and, as Al Burnett would say, 'Make Merry.'

MONDAY, 18 JUNE

A great weekend. On Friday night I told all the girls about my job. They were very impressed and I succeeded in getting Yvonne into bed at last. She is tough as an alley cat on the surface but quite scared underneath – like an alley cat is, I

---

* Lord Garrett Moore, later Earl of Drogheda, chairman of the *Financial Times*.
** Joan Carr, a concert pianist.
*** A nightclub run by a comedian called Al Burnett. The clientele was largely made up of rich young men of a type now known as 'Hooray Henrys'.

suppose. She is really too moody for me, but she was just the company I needed to stop me getting big-headed. After all, I'm not exactly going to direct MM in a movie yet.

I had quite a hangover on Saturday, but I spent Sunday sleeping in the garden and today I felt really good.

This morning Mr P gave me quite a cheerful, for him, 'Hello Colin,' when he came in. Mind you, if you didn't know him, you'd have thought he was going to a funeral. He must have a wardrobe full of the same clothes as he never varies what he wears, day by day. Brown tweed suit, dark brown shoes, pale brown shirt, brown tie etc. Gilman said he'd never ever seen him in anything else. (There is a *Mrs* P. I wonder what she thinks?) After a bit, Mr P called me into the office.

'You might as well know everything we are doing if you are to be any use.'

He showed me a huge squared-off sheet of paper, covered in columns and names and shaded squares.

This is really Mr P's pride and joy, his *chef d'oeuvre*, his bible. It is called a cross-plot. It has been cunningly worked out so that Pinewood's studios A and B can be alternated, with different 'sets' being built on one stage while the other was being used for filming.

To get the most out of each set the film is not shot in chronological order. If there is a scene in a particular room at the beginning of the story and another scene at the end in the same room, then they will both be filmed together. This is especially hard for film actors who have to develop a character in fits and starts.

The major actors also have to be fitted into the cross-plot so that we get the most out of them in the shortest time. Dame Sybil Thorndike,* for instance, is going to play Sir Laurence's mother-in-law (no more 'Larry' now that I'm officially working

---

* (1882–1976). *Grande dame* of British stage and screen. She was the first actress to play Shaw's *St Joan* (1923).

for him). But she is also booked for a West End stage play, so all her scenes have to be shot first if possible and most should be finished before the play begins. (Some of her scenes need special effects and these can be put in later.) SLO* and MM and Richard Wattis** are in virtually all the scenes so they don't influence the cross-plot much.

MM has a terrible reputation for being late on the set, and not turning up at all on some days. Mr P has scheduled her to do all her scenes first with a long list of alternate shots, cutaways and reactions which can be put in at short notice if MM is not available.

'What happens if shooting gets a week behind? The whole plan will collapse.'

Mr P grinned a Machiavellian grin and pulled out a second sheet and a third.

'We just switch sheets. Warner Bros will never know.'

I gather that Warner Bros is lending LOP and MMP the money to make the film. Already I hear Mr P say: 'Charge it to MMP' pretty frequently. I wonder if MMP is MM herself, or a group of people backing her.

I don't dare ask anything about MM. It seems in bad taste, like asking about childbirth. Anyway my job is to be preparing for MM's arrival. Police, press, chauffeur, bodyguard, servants, redecorations, everything to delight her eye and soothe her nerves. She must be a very difficult lady. I can't believe anyone is so unreasonable and silly, that they have to be spoiled so much. What would Nanny have said?

---

* i.e. Sir Laurence Olivier. When filming began the whole crew was to use this abbreviation.
** (1912–75). He was playing Mr Northbrook of the Foreign Office in the film.

TUESDAY, 19 JUNE

Six weeks until filming starts and a lot to prepare. Mr P depends on me a lot now but of course he won't need me at all when it does. Today a David Orton came in, and Mr P warned me that on him my future in the production would depend. He is going to be 1st Assistant Director. This does not mean SLO's assistant (SLO being the director), but the man in charge of seeing that everyone in the studio does what they are told.

'He's a sort of sergeant major,' explained Mr P.

This didn't sound very attractive and I can't say I liked him at all. Blondish-mousy hair, a thin face and glasses which he is forever pushing up onto the bridge of his nose with his fore-finger. He did not take to me either:

'Have you worked on a film before?'

'No.'

'Then forget it. If you haven't made a film already then you aren't in the union, and there is no way in which you can work on a film, in any capacity.'

Very funny! It seems the union is the ACT, the Association of Cinematograph Technicians, and they are a famous 'closed shop'. (No card, no film; no film, no card.)

So Mr Orton advised me to stay in Mr P's office. This is very disappointing. Mr P has already told me I can't stay in his office after production begins. And anyway I want to be a film *director*, not producer.

Mr P cheered me up by telling me to go down to see Diana Dors'* house tomorrow. It is somewhere near Ascot or maybe Henley. I've only got the phone number so far. Her agent has learned that MM is looking for something for the summer and thinks it might be good publicity if they could swap houses.

---

* 1931–84, real name Diana Fluck. Popular British actress whose many films included *Good Time Girl*, *Lady Godiva Rides Again*, *Passport to Shame* etc.

Of course we already have two houses, for MM and her manager, but I suppose some other creeps like APJ might arrive from America so I'll go and look.

Diana Dors always seems very sexy, even if extremely common. A bit of a tart.

WEDNESDAY, 20 JUNE

Diana Dors is divine. She's as vulgar and cheeky as I imagined from her films, but with a hilarious sense of humour. She never stops cracking jokes and telling stories. Her conversations peppered with F—s and C—s.

Her house is near the river, although I couldn't see it, as she has a huge indoor pool. She and a starlet friend were sitting by the pool in bikinis when I arrived. DD is smaller than you would think in real life. I suppose the camera exaggerates her on purpose. She is quite a pretty girl, and her friend was even prettier but not so vivacious. DD could not care less about the house swap but she did want to hear about MM. It was quite a let-down when I was forced to admit that I hadn't met MM yet. DD got bored very quickly, so to liven things up she and her friend both took off their bikini tops and jumped into the pool. That got my attention all right. There were two workmen hammering at something at the far end and their eyes stood out like organ stops. They just downed tools and stared.

Both girls have beautiful, quite small breasts but I must admit that they were so brazen that I was more embarrassed than rapacious. They must have been on the game together in the old days, is my guess.

The house is much too small for MM or her retinue, and has no class at all. With this film, MM is trying to go up in the world, not down. So I left silently and reported back to Mr P. He just chuckled. He hates film stars really.

THURSDAY, 21 JUNE

Thank goodness, I was completely wrong about David Orton. Underneath that severe exterior he is a very nice man. He is just awkward with people until he knows them.

He is married to a pretty, jolly make-up girl called Penny, who picked him up this evening. His world is the film studio, where he is in charge of course, and he is very experienced. He gave me a long explanation about how film studios work. Like in every job, there is a hierarchy which is very important. This is true in each department – the lighting cameraman is head of one group, and pretty much above everyone except the director, the designer has his crew – set-dressers, down to chippies (carpenters); there is wardrobe, make-up, film editing etc., each with their own structure. The Director has an Associate Director, but his right-hand man is the 1st Assistant Director – David in our case.

The lowest of the low is the *3rd* Assistant Director who is known as a 'gofer'. Anyone can tell him to 'go for this, go for that'.

This is the job he'll try to get for me, but even a 3rd Ast Dir needs a union card and that is the hardest thing in the world to get: actually it is the same card as a director needs to work on a film, but it is a different grade. David has promised to try and come up with a scheme to get round the union 'closed shop' rule. I trust him.

Mr P has other worries and so has SLO. I'm not surprised. I saw the play on which the film is going to be based: *The Sleeping Prince*. Larry and Vivien did it together – at the Phoenix Theatre in 1953–4* – and it was a very slight piece indeed.

* Vivien Leigh had created the role of Elsie Dagenham, changed to Elsie Marina when Marilyn played her in the film.

Typical Rattigan* – theatrical, charming and that's all. Vivien was enchanting as ever, despite a funny accent. But I thought Larry was at his worst. He has an old-fashioned notion that it is funny to play European royalty, and he gets wooden and mannered. The whole play ended up like a sort of 1930s in-joke – hardly Hollywood. I can't see it being a good role for MM. I suppose she thinks it will enhance her new 'intellectual' image. She will certainly have been told what a fantastic opportunity it is to play opposite the greatest classical actor of the generation etc. But Rattigan is no Shakespeare. Unless MM is cleverer than she looks, she will find it jolly hard to mix her style with Olivier's. She is said to be reading Dostoevsky or *War and Peace* or something so maybe she will surprise us all. Diana Dors surprised me, but she's more a crafty cockney than an intellectual.

FRIDAY, 22 JUNE

SLO came in, in quite a state. Problems already. After a bit I was called in to Mr P's office to 'join the discussions' – providing I do not speak unless asked a direct question! It seems that MM is going to marry Arthur Miller** this weekend. What sort of an effect will that have on her? And on the production? Will Miller persuade her not to come, and whisk her off on a glamorous honeymoon? SLO says he is a self-satisfied, argumentative, pseudo-intellectual. Charming. Will he help MM or make her argumentative too? She has a dreadful reputation already among movie directors. She is always late on the set, often does not show up for days on end, and can never remember her lines. What on earth can be the matter?

* Terence Rattigan (1911–77). Popular West End playwright (*The Winslow Boy, The Browning Version, Separate Tables* etc.).
** b.1915. American playwright (*The Crucible, Death of a Salesman, A View from the Bridge* etc.).

Her producer, and the co-producer of the film, with SLO, is called Milton Greene.* It is for him that I have rented Tibbs Farm. He will be responsible for MM while she is here, making sure she does turn up and keeping an eye on the expenses. But it seems he does not like Arthur Miller. He got MM out of her 20th Century contract, together with a lawyer called Irving Stein.** Evidently Milton Greene has given SLO his assurance that he can make MM behave herself.

After all it is her own money that is involved this time. Marilyn Monroe Productions (MMP) has a big share in the profits, just like LOP. If MM doesn't turn up for work, then she (and her partners, Greene and Stein***) start losing money. That is the theory. I don't know if it has occurred to any of them that while the three men involved (MG, IS and AM) want money, MM may be more interested in her career, but I didn't dare say so. Poor SLO. He is already upset enough. He doesn't trust any of the Americans and is out of his depth.

'What have I got myself into, Colin?'

'I think it will be a fantastic success, Larry,' I replied (using Larry for the last time, I swear it).

Mr P beamed in the background. His prodigy had said the right thing. 'Success for her or success for me?' said SLO but he was comforted for the moment (so easily?!).

And on top of AM there is the problem of the Strasbergs.† Lee Strasberg is the head of the Actors' Studio in New York, where MM sometimes studies (like once??). He is her god. He doesn't want to come over to London and desert his other

* Milton Greene (1922–85) was a fashion and celebrity photographer who had formed Marilyn Monroe Productions with Marilyn Monroe a year previously.

** Stein, Chairman of the Elgin Watch Co., was killed in a car accident in 1966.

*** Stein was not in fact a partner.

† Lee Strasberg (1899–1982) founded the Actors' Studio, famous for teaching 'the Method'. He went on to act, brilliantly, in films such as *The Godfather Part Two*. His wife Paula had been an actress.

students so he is sending over his wife, Paula. Paula Strasberg is a famous menace. As MM's 'drama coach' she could undermine SLO.

Naturally SLO wants a professional actor's approach. MM learns the role and decides how to play it; SLO makes suggestions, they discuss them, MM alters her performance accordingly etc. What will Paula's approach be? How will she fit in between them?

Throughout all this, a new idea has occurred to me. A couple of years ago, Lee and Paula's daughter Susan completely stole my heart in a film called *Picnic*. Susan played the kid sister of a blonde called Kim Novak. KN was meant to be the beautiful one and SS the ugly duckling – aged about 15, I suppose. Needless to say SS was 100 times more attractive than Novak in every way. I am a complete sucker for little skinny girls with big brown eyes. At the time I fell in love with Susan Strasberg, I had only just got over Pier Angeli marrying some dreadful Hollywood crooner.* I could hardly stop myself from asking whether Paula was bringing her daughter with her. I suppose not, but with luck, Susan might *visit* her Mum.

Anyway, I kept quiet.

Mr P and SLO had a long moan about Hollywood and Hollywood types and agents, lawyers, producers, stars. I don't think SLO is jealous. After all he and Vivien have both had huge Hollywood successes. He just can't stand the lack of professionalism. He sees 'the Method', which originates in New York, of course, but influences all the new Hollywood stars, as an excuse for self-indulgence.

Everyone is seduced by MM's particular form of glamour and SLO fears he has fallen into a trap. MM is not like any leading lady he's ever known and he can't fathom it. He can't

---

* Pier Angeli: Italian actress, modestly successful in Hollywood in the fifties and sixties, who committed suicide in 1971, aged thirty-nine. She was married to the singer and actor Vic Damone.

figure out whether she has a brain in her head or not. He knows he's a very attractive man, but she doesn't seem to have really noticed him. She only sees his reputation. She'll be here in three weeks and then we'll find out.

It's true that I don't think of SLO as a movie star, despite *Henry V* and all the films he's made. I think of him as a great actor. How will a 'star' and an actor mix. They'll have to find somewhere to meet between the sky and the stage.

I know I want to be a professional, like SLO. If I get a job on the film, I must stick to him like glue!

MONDAY, 25 JUNE

The whole office is busy planning for MM's arrival. Frequent directions arrive from America about the colours she likes, the materials she likes, the decorations she likes. The dressing-room suite at Pinewood is to be all beige. In fact beige is the only colour everyone agrees is safe. Red is out. Blue is out. Green is out. It is as if these colours were enemies.

Garrett and Joan are having the master bedroom suite at Englefield Green repainted white. They say they hate beige and won't change it. I told them I was having their village renamed Englefield Beige. For the money we (well, MMP to be accurate) are paying them, they could repaint the whole house many times over, but Garrett is too mean.

I made an appointment for Thursday with the police at Heathrow Airport to plan MM's arrival on 14 July. The Inspector thought I was kidding at first. But when I threatened 3000 fans he took me seriously.

Evidently when the crooner Johnny Ray came through, he – the Inspector – had his little finger broken in the mêlée. Johnny Ray's publicity people had gone down to the East End and filled up four buses with slum teenagers. They gave each one 10 shillings to cause as much pandemonium as possible when Ray appeared. This they duly did, and Johnny Ray's arrival was instant front-page news.

The Inspector says if we plan something like this he will personally have me arrested. I assure him that SLO himself has entrusted me with the job of getting MM into the country as discreetly as possible. He is still doubtful but I can tell that even he cannot resist the chance of meeting MM in the flesh. Her name has a magic effect.

People who are going to be associated with the production of the film drift in.

Roger Furse* is going to be the designer. I have met him before with Vivien – I think at Notley. He always seems to have a hangover, never stops smoking. He ran out of Capstans and cadged three of my Woodbines. (I never get time to smoke anything larger.) Mr P won't allow me to smoke in his office, despite his continual pipe puffing. I find Roger very sympathetic but Mr P clearly does not.

'Never trust the dirty fingernail brigade, Colin,' he said after Roger had left. 'They pretend to be only doing it for their art, but they are always trying to wangle more money.'

I took a quick squint at my fingernails – not that clean. I need the job, not the money, but I suppose that I must admit I am prepared to wangle.

My worry is that Roger is rather too 'stagey'. The more SLO surrounds himself with stage people, the more 'stagey' the film will be. Perhaps that's the intention – to make the film a sort of period piece – rich, theatrical and far from MM's normal image.

Jolly hard to pull off though. SLO may like it and MM may like it, but will filmgoers pay to see it?

* Furse (d.1972) had also designed the stage sets for the London production of *The Sleeping Prince*.

TUESDAY, 26 JUNE

Another 'old friend' today.

Tony Bushell* roared in at 12.30 to meet SLO and Rattigan for lunch. Tony looks like a bluff military man – bald, red faced and jovial. In fact he was in the Guards during the war and almost everyone forgets he is an actor.

David Niven told Mama that when Tony applied to join some grand regiment, the Adjutant asked him what he did for a living.

'Nothing at the moment,' said Tony, who, like all actors, was out of work.

'Thank goodness,' said the Adjutant, assuming Tony was idle rich, 'I thought you might be an actor. The last actor chappie we had ran off with the Colonel's wife.'

So Tony got in, and sure enough, ran off with the wife of someone in the regiment.

Very adorable she is too. Anne Bushell is a great friend of Vivien's, as Tony is of SLO's. In fact Anne talks exactly like Vivien (though she is not an actress at all – she is an heiress), and when she answers the phone at Notley one can't tell the difference. She is not as beautiful as Vivien (no one is) but she is still very attractive – as well as a good deal easier to be with.

Tony boomed a great welcome to me. He is going to be the Associate Director. This means that while SLO is acting in *front* of the camera, Tony will take charge *behind* it, and 'direct' the film.

I don't think Tony could direct traffic in Cheltenham. Despite his imposing appearance he is really a pussy cat. But SLO needs a chum to guard his rear, as it were, and it is a great joy to

* b.1904. Actor in Hollywood and British films of the 1930s (*Disraeli, Journey's End, The Scarlet Pimpernel* etc.) who later became a producer. He had worked with Olivier on the films of *Hamlet* (1948) and *Richard III* (1956).

have Tony around. He has a heart the size of a house which he loves to hide behind a glare. I've met Rattigan too, but he didn't remember me. He's queer of course, although I've nothing against that. He's charming to everyone but with a cautious look in his eye. I can't pretend I think he's much cop as a writer. Very 1920s period stuff. Of course, there's always an edge but if there wasn't even that his plays would just be blancmange.

SLO and Vivien probably know this but they love to have queer courtiers, and Rattigan's plays are quite good vehicles for actors.

They all went off to the Ivy in high good spirits. Like a lot of overgrown schoolboys, I thought.

'Hmph' said Mr P as we settled down to the cheese rolls and Guinnesses – which I buy and we now consume together in his office.

WEDNESDAY, 27 JUNE

Mr P has finally admitted that MM may need a bodyguard. The newspapers are making such a fuss of her and the upcoming visit. You would think that her fans are massing at strategic points to trample her to death in the rush for her autograph. 'Phooey' we say, but we can't take risks, and anyway the cost will come out of MMP's budget.

Mr P has no idea how to arrange a bodyguard so I rang Scotland Yard. When I finally got through to someone senior enough, they were incredulous and angry.

'Miss Marilyn Monroe will be adequately protected by the police while in this country like every other American visitor,' said some Commissioner sniffily. I patiently explained that if there was a retired Inspector around who would like to spend four months in Miss Monroe's company for a high salary I would like his name.

Once again the magical MM image made a strong man wilt. In fact I think the Commissioner sounded as if he might resign there and then to take the job. (Imagine what he could tell the wife – line of duty and all that.) He would have someone call me in the afternoon. And he did call – a real Inspector Plod. He was cautious and realistic – quiet sense of humour, not overawed. Sounds just what Mr P and I need. I invited him to come here to meet us in a week's time.

Tomorrow I'm going to Heathrow to see those police. (I may mention Plod's name.) It's to be a conference. I am afraid they are expecting someone older than me but it can't be helped. I'll just have to play the officer to the hilt. The RAF wasn't exactly the Life Guards, but I do know how. Most of those senior cops are just sergeant-majors at heart. As soon as they realise that I am serious, they'll settle down.

THURSDAY, 28 JUNE

The police at the airport were very suspicious. They assumed that I had come out there to arrange some sort of publicity stunt. Luckily I have experience of this sort of planning – defending Dalcross airport against infiltration* – and I managed to get their interest. Which corridor, which car park, which tunnel etc.

SLO really does want a very low-key reception for MM. He and Vivien will come to meet her. The press can have a short question and answer session plus pictures in a room especially set up between immigration and the cars. MM and AM have to go through Immigration and Customs, no matter what, but the police have promised to whisk them through alone.

So together we planned the whole thing like a military manoeuvre. I ended by telling them not to alter our plan in any way unless advised by me. (Milton Greene and Irving Stein

* While stationed there in the RAF in 1952.

and some publicity types are coming in ahead of MM and Mr P says that they are certain to try to change everything.)

In the end the cops became great chums. They all want to be the one who stands next to MM and protects her from the mob. She has that effect on all men, I guess. They certainly do not want a riot in their airport. Memories of Johnny Ray are all too recent. I was very Old Etonian Guards officer visiting the Sergeants' Mess, even though they are in black tunics covered in silver braid. But we understood one another.

David Orton came in again this afternoon. He gets nicer and nicer, and receives my plaintive enquiries about a job with twinkles and winks.

'Wait until next week. It's the middle of summer, you know.'

What can that mean? I know it is summer. It is extremely hot. But I trust him to help. I'm very lucky that he has become a friend.

FRIDAY, 29 JUNE

Garrett Moore is being very difficult about Parkside House again. What about the phone bill? What about the mess and the possible damage? I keep telling him that it will only be MM, AM and a Scotland Yard detective – although in reality I'm none too sure about this. There are always hangers-on, but they are meant to be at Tibbs Farm.

The Moores' servants will stay on at the house for MM, paid by Garrett who will be recompensed by MMP. This way, Garrett hopes not to lose them. Garrett is like a child, whining about someone playing with his toys.* Joan says nothing – just smiles and flutters those amazing eyelashes. She is the most seductive woman since Cleopatra. She and Vivien are in the same mould only she is passive where Vivien is active. Joan is

---

* I later became fond of Garrett, and he was right about the house. AM and MM left a *very* large unpaid phone bill.

older of course, but when she plays the piano for a concert, most of the men in the audience are close to fainting. I suppose Joan and Vivien know each other – it's not the sort of question to ask either of them – probably through Papa: lucky old man. I would be putty in Joan's hands, but I have to be tough with Garrett. I'm sure he can't resist £120 per week and I'm sure he can't resist the slightest chance to get his hand up MM's skirt. I know he is meant to be so brilliantly clever, but he is also extremely vain.

Mr P is pleased by the airport arrangements and by the bodyguard, although we haven't met him yet. None of the film production crew will be put on salary until 23 July, and he depends on me to negotiate with Garrett and Mrs C-P.

The costume designer came in to arrange her contract. Beatrice 'Bumble' Dawson* is a jolly, ginny neurotic old bird who SLO has used many times. She smokes continuously and grinds her teeth. In an effort to conquer this last habit, she is trying to replace it with twisting a lock of hair, a psychoanalyst trick which results in simultaneous grinding and twisting! She laughs a lot, between puffs, and is very sympathetic.

I can see why SLO has chosen so many chums. It is going to make life in the studio very easy. But I wonder if MM and Co will appreciate that sort of atmosphere.

MONDAY, 2 JULY

MM finally married Arthur Miller in New England over the weekend. Nobody here knows if that is good or bad for the film. Rumour has it that she panicked at the last minute and tried to get out of it.

Just before the wedding, a car full of reporters chasing the

---

* b.1908. Her many designs for Vivien Leigh's costumes included *Caesar and Cleopatra*.

happy couple crashed and the *Paris Match* woman was killed. MM was very badly shaken and saw it as a bad omen – as if one was needed. The poor girl seems to invite disaster. Perhaps she *needs* calamity, so that she is permanently in that helpless condition from which everyone wants to rescue her. But SLO, and Mr P for that matter, do not see her in that light and have no desire to do so. SLO probably once thought the whole thing would be a bit of a lark. He could have fun, make money and add considerably to *his* glamour. SLO's charm can be devastating – but will it work on MM? Of course, Vivien loves SLO despite his charm, not because of it. She is very demanding of his time and his attention – almost to the point of obsession. But she always defers to him as the great actor and the great star – even though she won an Oscar first* and is really more famous.

Vivien makes it quite clear that she regards SLO as more important than her, but I wonder if this will help him in his dealings with MM. He must not be grandiose or condescending. MM is too big to be treated like that.

Richard Addinsell** came in this evening to talk about music. He is quiet and modest with a very good reputation for film music. SLO wants a catchy romantic melody for the theme of the movie. Evidently MM has agreed to sing it. She did sing in *Gentlemen Prefer Blondes* and she has a low husky sort of voice, slight but not unpleasant.

The question of how much music there will be in the film has still not been solved. Rattigan wants very little but SLO disagrees and MM wants lots.

Meanwhile Vivien – who created the role MM will play –

* For Scarlett O'Hara in *Gone with the Wind*, 1939. She was awarded a second Oscar for Blanche DuBois in *A Streetcar Named Desire*, 1951. Olivier won a Special Academy Award for *Henry V* (1944), and a second for Best Actor as *Hamlet* (1948).
** British composer (1904–77). His film scores included *Goodbye Mr Chips*, *Dangerous Moonlight* (including the 'Warsaw Concerto'), *Blithe Spirit* etc.

sides with Rattigan. I think the music might give the film another sort of appeal (i.e. to make up for the obvious deficiencies in Rattigan's script), but I couldn't say this, even to Mr P. The general line is that with SLO and MM in the same film, everyone will flock to see it since everyone is in love with one or the other. But the play seems to me a very doubtful vehicle for two great stars, and Rattigan is going to write the screenplay too. Perhaps enough people will go to see it out of curiosity. 'What on earth made him/her want to do a film with her/him?'

That's something I'm curious about too.

TUESDAY, 3 JULY

Dave Orton, first assistant director to be, has a plan to get me the job of third assistant director. He has a friend who works in the ACT union office. This friend is going to tell him when the number of unemployed 3rd Ast Dirs on the union books gets really low, which it does every summer. When there are only four or five left he will ring the union and ask for a 3rd Ast Dir right away. They will send him the list of names and he will say that none of them is suitable – which is probably true. Then he will tell them that he has a young man already working in the Production Office and ask them to issue a temporary card to him. This they will have to do, and then I can work on the film on a temporary card. Once the film is over, I will have done a film and can apply for a permanent card. This is the only way round the 'no film, no card; no card, no film' rule.

David is brilliant. He is a very nice man underneath that gruff exterior and rather like Mr P. Both of them expect their orders to be carried out to the letter.

Every morning when Mr P comes in he asks me: 'What's the first thing you do, Colin?'

'You check, Mr Perceval.'
'And what is the second thing you do?'
'You check again, Mr Perceval.'
'Grmph.'

I mentioned this to David who explained that the slightest mistake in the movie world, which causes filming to be delayed by even an hour, can cause chaos later and cost millions. Just imagine the problem if everyone made a little careless slip now and again – so no one must. Directors and producers only hire you if they can be absolutely sure you will get it right. This means that you must have a well prepared fall-back position just in case things do go wrong, even if it's not your fault. Eyes in the back of your head are a necessity not a luxury. Unlike in the Army, the blame will always fall on the lowliest person involved, and on this film that is going to be me. Never mind. I enjoy the challenge, and, for the first time, I think maybe I might have made the right decision not to do a fourth year at Oxford.

WEDNESDAY, 4 JULY

My policeman came for his interview today – first with me and then with Mr P. We have codenamed him PLOD to confuse the Yanks.

He is absolutely perfect. He looks like a favourite uncle. He has a great sense of humour but is very shrewd underneath. He only retired from the police force a few months ago, so he knows everyone in Scotland Yard. Thank goodness he is extremely unimpressed by the film world and even by MM's glamorous image. I made it clear that his principal duty was going to be to protect MM against photographers as well as lunatic fans. He gave a very wry grin and pointed out that it is not against the law to take a photograph of Miss Monroe, or anyone else.

'Yes, yes, protect her *person*,' I said, but of course he is right. Since he is to live in MM's house at Englefield Green, all expenses paid on a huge salary, he isn't going to refuse. Mrs Plod will have to put up with this somehow, he said with a chuckle. 'I hope she's jealous.'

I wheeled him in to Mr P, who loved him of course, since they both hate showbiz. Mr P made it clear that he trusted me to make the appointment, he just wanted to discuss the sensitive nature of the job. My eyebrows went up but Plod's didn't. (I suspect they never do.) Mr P grumbled and rumbled round the subject for a while but what emerged was that Plod's second duty was to act as a spy for LOP, with me as his contact. He would be the only person in Englefield Green whom we could trust for a commonsense report on what was going on there. MM was notoriously unreliable and unpredictable. Plod would be her shadow and could keep us informed, not of her private life of course (of course!) but of any developments which might affect the progress of the film. This would be immensely helpful on the mornings when she clearly had no intention of leaving the house. Then we could arrange for other things to film. Mr P explained that it would take 2½ hours every morning to put on MM's make-up, wig and costume. She had to be at Pinewood Studios by 7 a.m. if filming was to start at 9.30 a.m. This meant that she had to leave Englefield by 6.30 a.m. 'Laurence will arrive at 6.45 a.m. promptly, Colin, and you will already be there to greet him,' Mr P said gravely.

On the days that MM had decided not to come at all, if we could be made aware of that by, say, 7.30, we could switch the schedule round to film shots without MM in them. Even these needed a couple of hours to set up and light, so every minute was vital.

Plod took all this in with a few gruff chuckles. I don't think Mrs Plod needs 2½ hours to do her hair and make-up in the morning. (I have known ladies take all day.) The other thing

Plod had to do was sign a document swearing that he wouldn't sell information to the newspaper. I think quite a few people have to sign this as Mr P had the form typed and ready. I haven't had to sign anything. I'm sure (I hope) he knows by now that I am absolutely loyal to SLO and him.

Plod will start next Monday, 9 July – and I will take him round and show him all the relevant addresses then. Someone from the Legal Department at Pinewood has contracted Parkside and Tibbs from then on, so Plod can move in if necessary. He is a very honourable man, and I think he will be a great ally.

THURSDAY, 5 JULY

Mr P and I went down to Pinewood Studios in a hired car. We didn't tell the driver but he was on trial for the job as MM's chauffeur. I think he will be perfect. He is very stupid, and never shows any emotion at all. The car, an Austin Princess, has a glass division and normally Plod will ride up front with the driver, while MM rides in the back. I wonder if AM will come to watch his bride filming, or stay in his study and write plays.

Pinewood is guarded by a studio police force which is hell-bent on keeping out the press and other intruders. Every vehicle is checked at the gate just like in the RAF. Once inside there are three huge studios joined by a very long concrete corridor. The other side of this corridor are the star dressing rooms, crowd dressing rooms, make-up rooms, wardrobe rooms etc. Across a little private road is the club house, with bars and a restaurant. MM's and SLO's dressing rooms are going to be at the end of one of the side corridors, opposite the restaurant. It really is all very like an RAF base with its hangars, offices and officers' mess.

We are going to alternate between Studios A and B while

other minor British films are being made in Studio C. There is a large 'lot' for filming outside scenes, but our film doesn't have many of these as far as I can see.

Mr P and I first inspected MM's dressing-room suite. Filming doesn't start for four weeks but she must have somewhere suitable to relax in when she comes for rehearsals in three weeks' time.

We were shown a series of what looked like old cowsheds which made me anxious.

'Don't worry Colin. The scene builders and set dressers only need 48 hours to convert this into the Dorchester. We are just here to check which ones have been allotted to us.'

We were shown round by Teddy Joseph, the production manager to be, who is still working on another film here at the moment. Small, bespectacled, a bit like a penguin, he will be Mr P's right arm when filming starts. Teddy showed me round the various departments. We will use Pinewood facilities for everything but the stars.

In the wardrobe department was one of the prettiest little girls I have ever seen in my life. This is very good news indeed since I am going to be working here myself for four months. Slim as a wand, curly brown hair, huge brown eyes and a wide cheeky grin. The head of the department is a large motherly lady. She definitely feels that it is her duty to protect her little lambs from prowling 3rd Ast Dirs. But the 'wand' was thrilled to bits. After all I was with Mr P – and Mr P is supreme boss, at least until SLO arrives. Teddy persuaded Mr P that all was well, Mr P caught me by the ear to prevent me bobbing up to Wardrobe for the sixth time and we returned to London. Pinewood strikes me as a bastion of professionalism and common sense. It is not at all like the Hollywood studios I have read about. With Teddy and David and Tony Bushell in charge, what can go wrong?

FRIDAY, 6 JULY

Last night I asked myself what could go wrong. Today the whole movie seemed in question, before the camera has even rolled. A rumour came from the USA at lunchtime that AM was going to have his passport refused after all.* This would mean that he couldn't come to London, and MM would certainly not come to London for four months without him. Since huge sums of money have been spent already, this caused quite a panic. Everyone was on the phone, asking for reassurance which we could not give. Rattigan was especially put out. SLO was grim-faced and terse, firmly shutting me out of the office for his conference with Mr P and Tony B, and a series of calls to the USA.

No one could get through to MM and AM, but Milton Greene, on the transatlantic phone, was calm. It could be fixed, he was sure. But *he* couldn't find Irving Stein who had been with MM last night or speak to MM and Arthur at least. So the worrying went on all day.

Mr P has heard (from her last director) that MM often gets 'confused'. Surely he doesn't mean 'drunk'? Pills, more likely – as with Judy Garland. That may be the problem now, although I hope she isn't taking pills on the first week of her honeymoon. I suggested this to Mr P and got a very grumpy 'grmph'. But by 6 p.m. it was all solved. AM and MM had got up at last – 1 p.m. in the USA – and switched the phone on. Milton Greene was on the line to MM and SLO simultaneously and all was sweetness and light.

'Not a very good omen,' said Mr P, for the second time this week, as we finally left the office at 7 p.m. But he is always

---

* Miller had been under investigation by Senator McCarthy's House Un-American Activities Committee. His marriage to MM evidently convinced them that he was a regular guy.

pessimistic. I'm really relieved that the film is on the rails again. Gilman whisked Tony and SLO off to Notley in the Bentley. Anne had been waiting for them in the car. My goodness, she is an attractive woman, and extremely nice too. She gave me a great welcome, as if I was an old friend. But she is not in the least seductive, unlike Vivien. I'm off for a weekend in the country too – but alone. I sure envy those two men their beautiful ladies. I wouldn't mind staying in bed till 1 p.m. like Arthur Miller if I was with either of them – or both!

MONDAY, 9 JULY

Back to earth. SLO started to distribute cigarettes when he came in this morning. He is delighted that they have named a new cigarette after him, and now he gets free packets of 'Oliviers' for life. I suppose I didn't look as thrilled as I might have at this news so he told me quite sharply that the same tobacco company had named a cigarette after the great actor du Maurier.* He could hardly refuse.

'Oh of course, yes, wonderful,' I cried, but to me the idea of someone as great as SLO advertising something is a shame. Du Maurier was of another era – and probably needed the money which SLO does not. I know nothing about du Maurier but I think of him as an old ham, although quite unfairly I'm sure. More importantly, du Maurier cigarettes are not a great success.

SLO went on to explain that his costume in the film has no pockets so he wants me to be on call holding the cigarettes at all times in case he wants to smoke. I am naturally to smoke 'Oliviers' also, and I can get as many as I want from Gilman, who has crates of them.

After one day's trial I don't like them that much – I prefer

* Sir Gerald du Maurier (1873–1934).

Woodbines – but that isn't the point. 'On call by SLO's side at all times' is what I wanted to hear, and have been planning to be anyway. As soon as the film starts, my pay goes up to union scale (£10.10s. pw), I get free cigarettes, and I have to be at the director's side at all times. Good news.

I told this, with glee, to David Orton who came in at 4.30.

'The hell with that idea!' he roared. 'You work for me and me alone and don't you forget it. You are my slave. I don't want my 3rd Ast Dir poncing around with the director, even if it is SLO.'

'Quite right, David. I was only kidding.'

I've managed situations like this before, and it's nice to be in demand. Just a matter of being very quick on the feet and polite at all times.

Irving Stein and Milton Greene arrive from NYC tomorrow on the overnight flight. I offered to go to meet them but Mr P said 'no'. He's sent the chauffeur.

'Let the buggers find their own way around,' he growled.

Do I sense hostility to our American cousins already?

TUESDAY, 10 JULY

Milton Greene and Irving Stein are both very young. They came in like a couple of recent graduates from some Jewish university. Both were exhausted after the flight and looked wary, but very charming. Irving is more aloof; Milton more boyish, very slight, dark brown eyes always smiling. They must be extremely shrewd to have got control of the most famous film star in the world.

Milton masterminded the plot to break MM's contract with 20th Century and 'set her free'. I suppose these two are the up-and-coming Louis B. Mayers.

SLO was brimming over with bonhomie – always a bad sign. When he is irascible is when he is sincere. Milton treats me like an executive, which is nice! He asked me all the details of the houses, the servants, Plod and the airport reception.

SLO absolutely promised Milton that Vivien and he would be on hand 'to welcome Marilyn and Arthur' and join in the press conference.

'But let's keep it low key, old boy.'

SLO wants the minimum publicity of course, and Milton says he does too. I wonder if both men have the same definition of 'minimum'. I suspect SLO really means 'none' and Milton means 'front page of every paper in the world – but no scandal'. There is a new publicity man around who has been ringing newspapers all day – ostensibly to notify everyone about the press conference even though this has already been done by the Pinewood press office.

Whenever they have a chance, Milton and SLO go into very private conference, talking fast and low. 'MM worries' I suppose, that even Mr P and I are not allowed to know about.

WEDNESDAY, 11 JULY

Milton rang from Tibbs Farm – could we all go down there for lunch. He was tired after the flight. Mr P was delighted. He is more curious than he lets on! I drove down in the Bristol, behind Mr P and Tony in the Princess. That way Milton can meet the chauffeur MM will have. SLO met us there as it is nearer Notley. Everyone agreed that Tibbs is perfect – out of Milton's earshot that is. Nouveau-riche – bathrooms smelling of pot pourri and towels so thick and soft that they don't even dry your hands. SLO gazed round in genuine horror. He is used to Vivien's exquisite taste.

Gilman said, 'This is a bit of all right, Colin,' loudly enough to embarrass me and please Milton who thinks it is typically 'English'.

There was a huge bunch of roses in the Bentley from Vivien which Gilman took through to the kitchen to find a vase. A buffet lunch had been prepared by the Cotes-Preedy cook – mainly reheated delicacies from the Ascot shop which I recognised from my stay here. Milton had ordered salad and cold white wine, which made it seem American. SLO had also brought a lot of Olivier cigarettes.

'I get them free, dear boy,' he said with much pride, but I don't think Milton smokes. Perhaps he is a health and fitness addict.

After lunch Milton and SLO went into conference again, this time allowing Mr P and Tony in too. I hope Mr P has some gossip for me later.

At teatime we drove over to Englefield Green to see Parkside House. The Moores have left and only the servants are waiting for MM and her party. Plod will move in on Friday and the chauffeur will live out. Parkside really is too pretty for words. It is right on the edge of Windsor Great Park and has its own private entrance to the Royal Gardens – or so I'm told. It is in quite different taste to Tibbs – much more elegant and feminine thanks to Joan. The master bedroom has been repainted white. I never saw it when Joan was in it. (I wish I had though!) Everyone was delighted. Milton praised me very highly for both houses and Mr P beamed, for once.

SLO hadn't come, of course. He'd been to the house as a guest of Garrett and Joan's. I don't think SLO likes Garrett any more than I do. Garrett is famous for sneering at people less clever or less titled than himself – which means pretty well everyone. I must admit that I am pleased with the arrangements so far, but everyone warns me that the day MM arrives, the rules will all change. She is the most famous woman in the world, though, so I would expect her to be pretty wilful. The worst thing is to have all that clout and not know your own mind. If she says her favourite colour is beige, that has to be a definite possibility. Then she will be as dangerous as a Chinese Empress. We'll see in three days' time.

THURSDAY, 12 JULY

The press are really getting worked up about MM's impending arrival. They phone me up hourly, demanding interviews with MM and SLO. I tell them that there will be a press conference at the airport and another at the Savoy Hotel on Sunday but of course they already know this and they want more. Any request for MM has to go through the loathsome Arthur P. Jacobs who is coming back to the Savoy tomorrow. It isn't that MM wants to avoid publicity – publicity more than anything else has got her where she is. But you have to control how much money you print. Even publicity has to be rationed out to get the maximum effect. APJ is meant to be the expert on this.

But there is a new publicity/personal relations man who is very nice. He is an Englishman, who nevertheless works from Hollywood, called Rupert Allan* and he is the opposite to APJ, quiet, dignified, polite. Perhaps he acts as the antidote to APJ's type of poison.

MM's personal make-up man has also flown in. He came in to the office this morning, unannounced, 'just to say "Hi" '. His name is Allan Snyder but 'Call me Whitey' is his opening remark to everyone. Impassive, and courteous, he is a great contrast to the Hollywood types we were expecting. Evidently he used to be a great influence on MM and is still a great friend. She insists on his presence on each of her films. I wonder if he was ever her lover, too. In our case, he only has a limited work visa so he is doing her original make-up and then someone English will take over. Frankly I wish he was staying for the

* Allan (b.1913) was actually an American educated in England. He was the grandest personal publicist in Hollywood: his clients included Marlene Dietrich, Grace Kelly and Bette Davis.

whole movie. He has a wonderfully calming presence which could be a great help. But he clearly doesn't want to stay more than a few weeks anyway.

'I love Marilyn,' he said with a nice open grin, 'but I do not want to find myself responsible for her behaviour.'

Now he has wandered off to explore London. He gives no address and simply says he will see us at Pinewood next Tuesday. Even Mr P, who deeply distrusts all Americans, seemed to like him. I hope he doesn't come to any harm in Soho! He is probably not as naive as he seems.

FRIDAY, 13 JULY

Mr P's distrust of Americans was justified. Arthur Jacobs went to London Airport and changed all our careful plans for MM's arrival tomorrow. Once again the police there assumed the worst, jumping to the conclusion that all we all want is maximum disruption and publicity. In the end, one of them thought to telephone me. I didn't even know APJ was out there so I got very cross. I pointed out that they had promised to listen to no one but me; that APJ was a publicity man whose job was to get publicity whether his client wanted it or not; that SLO and MM's producers had both instructed me to arrange MM's arrival with minimum fuss etc. But the papers are nerving everyone up and the police are edgy.

Luckily APJ is so loud-mouthed and overbearing that they would much rather disobey him. I have promised to get there really early tomorrow morning and go over the details again. I do remember from the days of Gaby Pascal and Jean Simmons*

* Gabriel Pascal (1894–1954) was a Hungarian film producer who owned the screen rights to Bernard Shaw's works. He first had the idea of making *Pygmalion* into a musical (*My Fair Lady*, as it became). Jean Simmons (b.1929) appeared in his film versions of Shaw's *Caesar and Cleopatra* (1945) and *Androcles and the Lion* (1953). My sister and I spent the summer of 1948 with them in Venice.

that once show business retinues get on the move, it is very hard to influence them or deflect them. They are like rivers. They jolly well go where they want to, so you have to make the banks good and high. London Airport is very big and if we lose control there will be chaos. The police are efficient and charming, but like all men in uniform they will take orders from anyone in authority. It's going to be a close-run thing.

APJ did have one success out there, I must admit. So oogle-eyed are the junior cops about MM that four motorcycle riders have volunteered to escort her car from the airport to Englefield Green. Evidently that is an honour never granted to anyone before except visiting royalty. I hope MM is impressed. It is not the sort of thing SLO and Mr P meant by minimum fuss, but I must agree it sounds exciting.

SATURDAY, 14 JULY

The first problem was that it rained.

After all the fine weather we've had, a light rain was falling when I woke up and it got heavier. I got to the airport early and went straight to the police office to make everything as clear as possible. But within an hour APJ and his minions were there trying to make everything as confused as possible.

Milton Greene arrived, very nervous, and was all too ready to listen to APJ's panicky lies. Quite soon he too was trying to change the plans around. Rupert Allan also had ideas of his own, even if they were expressed a bit more calmly.

Luckily I had Plod on my side, and he could speak to the police in their own language. But he is so unflappable and monosyllabic that we often did not get heard.

As the time of arrival grew near, everyone began to get very crazy. MM is like Desdemona: 'It is the very error of the moon;

She comes more nearer earth than she was wont and makes men mad.'*

By the time the plane from New York actually landed there were reporters everywhere. The first I saw of them was a bunch of yelling waving men in raincoats in Immigration. The Customs officers had lost their heads and been swept away. I suppose the very thought of searching MM's person had been too much for them.

In the middle of this rabble stood Arthur Miller, teeth clenched on an unlit pipe, grinning like an amiable crocodile. The girl he had his arm around was unmistakably Marilyn Monroe. She looked so exactly like her publicity photographs – blonde hair, white face, scarlet lips in a pout – that it was hard to see the person. Added to this she had on huge very dark dark-glasses.

Poor woman. She must have been very tired after the flight. I suppose her life is permanent chaos. As for Jacobs, on whom she depends for help and guidance, he clearly had only one aim – namely to create the maximum confusion and even physical danger. Then he could step in and appear to save her from the very problems he himself had generated. In the blur of faces and cameras, he would be the only one she would recognise, and turn to with gratitude.

AM had clearly decided to grin whatever happened and be steered by the crowd. He recognised no one, not even APJ.

Milton Greene was too small to have any effect. Plod and I are total unknowns. We flung ourselves into the crowd and only added to the confusion.

Somehow the police managed to steer this whole mad rabble into the hall set up for the press conference where SLO and Vivien were waiting. I left the main group and went to defend Vivien, with Gilman, as the riot spread all over the room. MM

* *Othello*, Act V, Scene ii.

and AM were lifted bodily onto the podium, and I was glad to see one of the cops giving APJ a good jab in the solar plexus. (He later threatened to have all the police at Heathrow fired!) Everyone was shouting at once and MM just looked confused and frightened. Finally Rupert Allan got onto the stage and quietened them all down. He announced that MM would make a short statement and then leave for a private destination to rest, until the main press conference at the Savoy tomorrow. Then MM took off her dark glasses and gave that famous smile and every flash bulb in the room popped at once creating such a blinding flash that she put the glasses back on immediately.

In a breathy little girl's voice, MM said that she was very glad to be in England at last, with her husband (looking fondly at Arthur), and how excited she was to be making a film with SLO. SLO got up to reply but no one took any notice and they all started yelling questions at MM. So he gave up and we literally strong-armed it to the exit.

MM and AM got into the Princess with Milton and APJ and they swished off with the four motorbike policemen in dangerously close formation. SLO and Vivien got into the Bentley with Gilman and followed right behind. I had to go to get the Bristol with Plod so the press cars got in between us.

When we arrived at Parkside House the press were lined up outside the gate with the four cops preventing them from going in. Plod persuaded them to let us through and we found AM and MM and SLO outside the front door on the gravel. MM had meant to thank the police outriders but who had got in and was trying to interview her but that little creep Donald Zec of the *Daily Mirror*. How *did* he get past the others? Plod and I moved across to chuck him out, but he suddenly put his hand round MM's waist. His photographer jumped out of the shrubbery and 'flash', before they both raced off. I suppose MM is used to this sort of behaviour from total strangers, but it drove the pressmen at the gate crazy.

AM whispered in MM's ear, MM whispered to Milton and he nodded. Then he sent me over to the reporters to tell them they could all come up the drive for one last photo. MM and AM stood in the doorway and smiled, arm in arm, before disappearing inside. Plod and I followed and Milton introduced Plod (but not me) to MM and AM. I don't think MM took in a word, but as Plod is going to live in her house she will soon get used to him.

'Well, we are going to bed,' said AM with a huge leer.

I thought this pretty vulgar. I saw MM notice it without much pleasure, but she pretended not to catch on so perhaps she is smarter than she looks. AM certainly doesn't behave like America's most eminent intellectual. More like an overgrown schoolboy. But MM has a very appealing aura, even if physically she is not my type. A bit too exaggerated.

Before SLO left he had said: 'I hope things are better organised tomorrow.'

I'll do my best but I think that even he has underestimated the press hunger for MM.

SUNDAY, 15 JULY

Except for the large crowd outside – and who organised that I wonder – the press conference was orderly. In fact it was predictable and dull. SLO arrived without Vivien. He was already in a bad temper – nose out of joint, perhaps? Mr P came sniffing around to have a look at how things were going on and a squint at MM. Irving Stein and APJ were already there – what a pair. APJ had clearly lost centre stage to Milton, who arrived with MM and AM.

The Savoy Hotel had organised itself much better than the airport police. MM's party was 45 minutes late which allowed the flower of the nation's press corps time to make many ribald jokes. D. Zec was telling everyone who would listen that MM was a personal friend of his.

MM still had on her dark glasses and barely spoke above a whisper. AM mainly grunted past his pipe. I would say that they both had hangovers of several different kinds.

SLO made a speech of welcome, which I thought was a little bit patronising – although I'm sure not intentionally. Cecil Tennant,* SLO's agent, was also on the stage. He is a bit of a bully and interrupted most forcefully if he didn't like a question. Rupert Allan was much more diplomatic and more friendly. Tennant would not dream of acknowledging my presence, even though I am clearly attached to SLO's party. It is true that I'm pretty inferior but I don't like people who act as if they were 'superior'.

Plod seems to be happily installed at MM's right elbow. He is like a lovely gruff uncle and when MM finally wakes up, she will be jolly glad to have him. I notice that she gives her coat to AM and AM gives it to Plod, so AM has already seen the benefit.

It's a bit like starting a new school. Everyone has to settle down and find out who the other boys are.

MONDAY, 16 JULY

Very quiet day after the hectic weekend. Only Mr P, myself and Vanessa. We will leave the Tibbs group and the Parkside group to themselves, although I am sure there will be a lot of traffic between the two (about six miles). Everyone asks me: 'What's she like? Is she beautiful?'

Well, she certainly looks like Marilyn Monroe, and not all film stars do look like their image. She has got a cute smile, but so far she only turns it on for the cameras. Her figure –

* Cecil Tennant was to be killed in a motor accident in 1967, on his way home from Vivien Leigh's funeral.

and especially her bust – is fantastic but a little on the plump side. Problems – too much fakery: peroxide hair, dead white make-up, heavy lipstick, but that is her image. She looks confused too, lost, troubled. That's the MM image too, I know, but even when she's shut the door on the reporters, she still looks in distress, not just acting it.

She doesn't seem to be able to shrug off the image in private, to throw off her coat, slump down on the sofa and say: 'Phew, let's have a drink.'

She gazes at AM as if he is a superhero, but I don't think he is that nice. He's clearly very handsome and very attractive, but good hearted, no. And she hasn't really got anyone else to depend on. A girl like that really needs her mum, like Margot,* but I'm told her mum is in a bin.** Milton is clearly dependent on her, rushing round like all the others trying not to upset her, frightened of her even.

SLO is much too remote. He's going to be her director and that should be a close relationship, but he is quite clearly not in any way concerned with her personally. He is the supreme professional, expecting and assuming that everyone else will be professional too. (You can see why he and Vivien get on so well.)

MM does have the dreaded Strasbergs, one or both of whom are going to turn up any day now. (Their darling daughter Susan will not be coming for a month, I'm told. But Rupert Allan, who knows everything, says she is expected one day. Hooray – hope springs eternal.)

I wish SLO could be cosy with MM. He's strong and romantic with most women but he only gets 'cosy' with men.

Speaking of which, Tony B is now permanently installed.

---

* The ballerina Margot Fonteyn (1919–91), an old family friend, whose mother was omnipresent.
** MM's mother had been certified insane in 1934, and spent the rest of her life in various hospitals. She died in 1984.

He is delightful company, and he is going to be behind the camera most of the time. But I doubt if MM goes for that English charm stuff. She clearly adores the strong silent intellectual type, and Tony certainly isn't that. He is SLO's AdC at all times, and keeps his eye on him only.

I must admit it is exciting to be working on this production. The most famous film star and the most famous actor. But they should change the name. *The Sleeping Prince* always confuses people. They think I mean 'The Sleeping Princess', as in 'Sleeping Beauty', and they miss the slight Rattigan pun. If the film was called 'The Naughty Chorus Girl' it would be more dramatic and easier to explain, but I suppose that would be like the old MM image, the one she wants to shed.

TUESDAY, 17 JULY

Milton phoned in a nervous state. He has heard that MM's dressing room at Pinewood is not ready yet (true) and he wants to show it to MM tomorrow when she will be there for the make-up test. (This is what is called the screen test, which I always thought was an audition. MM hardly needs an audition since MMP own half the film.)

Mr P is grim because he was specifically told by Milton that MM would not need a full dressing-room suite until filming begins in three weeks' time; and the main dressing room isn't even hired yet. She would normally just go into a make-up room with Whitey and then go home. Teddy Joseph was reassuring however. The dressing-room suite will be 'made' today, and if necessary it can be used by someone else for three weeks and then done again.

I pointed out to Mr P that MM might not like the decor, and then it would have to be redone anyway.

'Hmph.'

It is true that Milton is a fusspot and a perfectionist, but then so is Mr P so he can't complain. At lunchtime I phoned Plod at Parkside.

'What are they up to?'

'Playing trains,' said Plod, with a chuckle.

I hope they are going to get to Pinewood Studios by 9.30 tomorrow morning. Whitey has created a new make-up to match her new hair (a wig, of course)* and her new image.

'We will be ready to leave here by 8.30,' said Plod. 'I heard her mention it to Mr Miller.'

So not only does she remember her appointments but also Plod overhears her doing so, which is very good news.

'You'll have to leave the house at 6.30 when filming starts,' I said. Another chuckle.

I will get to the studio by 8 a.m. to meet David. He is responsible for getting everyone to the right place at the right time, and it is time I did some work for him.

WEDNESDAY, 18 JULY

It goes without saying that she was late – but not very late, only half an hour. She seems to have a tendency to leave the house about the time when she is due to arrive at her next appointment.

Milton arrived early and was quite cheerful. He was very relieved to see Whitey. 'She'll be on time for *you*,' he grinned.

The dressing-room suite is beige of course, but very very pretty, like a film set in the 1930s. There is an anteroom and sitting room and bathroom, all covered with deep Wilton carpet. The curtains are permanently drawn shut, and low table lights give a soft glow. There are flowers everywhere – a big bouquet from SLO and Vivien in the front.

* MM's hairstyle was created by the famous Hollywood stylist Sidney Guilaroff. He flew in for a few days but did not mix with the British crew, except to instruct the film's hairdresser Gordon Bond.

Of course the studios themselves are very forbidding and I wish the sun had come out. It didn't look at all like California – more like RAF Dishforth.*

When MM did arrive we all got a shock – except Whitey, I suppose. She looked absolutely frightful. No make-up, just a skirt, a tight blouse, head scarf and dark glasses. Nasty complexion, a lot of facial hair, shapeless figure and, when the glasses came off, a very vague look in her eye. No wonder she is so insecure.

She bolted into her dressing room with Milton and Whitey and stayed there for 20 minutes. Eventually they coaxed her out, looking very tense indeed, and walked her to the small studio.

The whole idea is to film her first without make-up on, so she sat on a stool, under the bright lights, like a prisoner of war.

Milton spoke to her and SLO spoke to her but she did not listen. Then Jack Cardiff** stepped forward. Jack is going to be the lighting cameraman. He is very well known in the business, and has some excellent films to his credit – *The Red Shoes* etc. He is also very charming in a completely natural way. MM is smart enough to know that the lighting cameraman is the one who makes her look beautiful, but she clearly liked Jack as a person. He is kind and tolerant and doesn't put on that awful old public schoolboy charm that Englishmen so often think is the best thing.

I hope I can be natural too. At least I was in the RAF not the Guards. Of course MM never noticed me, but then why should she?

David Orton was in charge of the studio, and he's the Sergeant Major all right. He has a very loud bark when he wants

* Where I was stationed as a Pilot Officer in 1952.
** b.1914. He won an Academy Award for his work on *Black Narcissus* (1946), and later turned to directing.

quiet. After half an hour of filming from every angle, MM dived back into her dressing room and Whitey got to work. We had taken a whole reel of MM sitting there like a naked sausage and it was time for the transformation to take place.

'Three hours,' said Whitey cheerfully, so we went to lunch. SLO, Tony and Jack went to the restaurant, David and I to the canteen. Pinewood eating facilities are set up to look demo-cratic – everyone eats in the same place. In fact the wood-panelled restaurant with waitress service is set so deep in the canteen that the stars are very much apart from the hoi polloi. The prices alone keep everyone in their allotted place. David explained that he has already started his efforts to get me the temporary union card so that I can be 3rd Ast Dir. I can tell from his twinkle that he is going to be successful so I don't push it. David looks mild but he doesn't suffer fools gladly – like Mr P.

After lunch there was a long wait until MM emerged, now fully made up with her blonde wig and chiffon top. At first sight she had just changed from a slum kid to a huge gift-wrapped dolly, but that's Jack's problem. He started playing with the lights again, changing their filters and shutters until he was satisfied, and the camera whirred away. For some reason SLO put Tony in charge of the afternoon shoot. There isn't much to do I suppose but stand around and look as if you are in charge, and Tony is very good at that.

Plod and the Princess reappeared. MM had sent them and the driver back to Parkside, I suspect to look after AM. Then MM left at high speed, as if she was afraid of being kidnapped. She reminded me of General Franco when I saw him in Vigo last year.* Milton and Whitey went after her in Milton's car. I notice that Plod now carries MM's handbag!

We are all going to see today's film in the viewing theatre

* I had spent the previous summer in Portugal and Spain, and saw Franco arrive in the port of Vigo, where he was very unpopular.

here tomorrow morning, before more tests of make-up, wardrobe and wigs.

David says 8 a.m. again tomorrow.

This is fun.

THURSDAY, 19 JULY

MM late again but this time no one cared. Everyone was only thinking about the 'rushes' – the film that was shot yesterday. At 9.30 Milton and SLO led the way into the viewing theatre, and we all held our breath. Jack and Whitey had already seen it together, early on. They were looking pretty smug but said nothing. They were going to MM's dressing room to start her make-up again and discuss technicalities.

The film was magical, and there's no other way to describe it. The stuff we shot in the morning, although it resembled a police line-up mug shot, was quite heartbreaking. MM looked like a young delinquent girl, helpless and vulnerable under the harsh lights. The afternoon footage was even more extraordinary. What an incredible transformation. Now MM looked like an angel – smooth, glowing, eyes shining with joy (Jack's lights), perfect lips slightly parted, irresistible. Quite a few people had wandered in to look and they were stunned. We all fell in love there and then. Milton was triumphant. He and SLO rushed to MM's dressing room to tell her the news, although I suppose they could not exactly explain how very relieved they were.

The rest of us joined Bumble Dawson for the wardrobe test. Now it was her turn to be nervous. We had only seen MM wrapped in chiffon so far. She need not have worried. MM finally appeared in a long white dress that suited her perfectly. It made her walk with an amazing wiggle, but a wiggle which is somehow naive not brazen. It also showed just enough of the famous Monroe bosom.

Bumble made various tiny alterations and then announced that two more fittings would be needed to get it right. (These will be at Parkside.)

MM did some twirls for the camera, but this time no one held their breath and Jack hardly bothered to adjust the lights. We all know what it will look like – ravishing.

At the end of the day, I was the last to leave. SLO had gone back to Notley with Tony, in high good spirits, after calling everyone to tell them the news. I went over to the bar for a drink. It is out of bounds during the day but empty after 6 p.m. Sitting alone I saw Whitey Snyder quietly sipping Scotch so I joined him.

'What an amazing transformation,' I said.

'Nothing to it,' said Whitey in his calm Yankee accent. 'The camera just loves some people,' he explained, 'and it sure loves Marilyn. Look at Bogart. Funny little man you wouldn't notice in a crowd, but on camera . . . ! Look at Gary Cooper. Wonderfully tall and good looking, yes, but can't act for toffee and never even tries. Doesn't ever change his expression by a hair's breadth, and yet when you see him on camera, everyone with him seems to be overacting. Just born with the magic. And so is Marilyn. However confused or difficult she is in real life, for the camera she can do no wrong. I tell her that all the time but she doesn't believe me. And sometimes I feel like telling her directors – don't fuss her, don't tell her what to do, just let her rip.'

I can see that he is genuinely fond of MM. The only person I've met so far who is. I wish I could sit him down for a quiet chat with SLO, but that's out of the question.

FRIDAY, 20 JULY

Last day of the tests. This time the hairdressers had lots of wigs to try, but we ended up with the first choice which has been so successful.

MM arrived in the car with Milton. Clearly he is trying to reassert his control, which may have temporarily been taken over by AM. He never stops whispering into MM's ear. Is this the fashionable way of communicating with film stars in Hollywood?* We also ran a test to choose MM's stand-in. Jack chose a skinny little blonde who doesn't look a bit like MM to me – no more a real blonde than MM either, I would guess. But it is Jack who will have to light her every day to get the set ready for MM, and he mumbled something about 'perfect skin tones'. Hmm. Who is perfect is the little Wardrobe girl. She could not be cuter or more flirtatious, and I made many more visits to the Wardrobe Department than were strictly necessary.

I hope David hasn't noticed. I didn't have the nerve to ask her out this weekend, but I stressed that I would be back on Monday and come to see her again then. I definitely have to get my hands on her!

I have had to learn my way around the studios in a hurry. David is always telling me to check something at one end or fetch someone from the other, and I spend a lot of time dashing along that long concrete corridor. Before the camera rolls, or 'turns over', a bell rings, red lights flash and the soundproof studio doors are locked automatically. It seems like an age if you are the wrong side of the doors, but actually the camera never runs for more than a minute or so. It is stopped between 'takes' to save film and it is returned to its starting position if it has been moved.

David told me that for the filming, there will be two 2nd Ast Dirs on call, one in the office and one in the studio. However that will not alter my role as his slave: I do not work for *anyone* else (except for SLO, Tony, Milton, Mr P and Vivien, think I).

Tomorrow I'm going down to the country for the weekend, to boast about MM.

* Yes it was, and still is.

MONDAY, 23 JULY

We were all at Pinewood again today, this time to listen to the music, which has been specially written by Richard Addinsell. SLO, Milton, Tony B, Terry Rattigan, David and I were all crammed in a rehearsal room. RA hummed and sang the main song he had written, accompanying himself on the piano. He is a very gentle, sympathetic man and we were all on his side. I'm not musical and I find it extremely hard to catch a tune the first time I hear it played. I remember M and D playing us the record of *My Fair Lady* when they came back from New York after attending the first night. The songs that had brought the house down in a live performance left us unmoved until we had played the record several times. It was the same now. Out of nerves, RA had put in so many decorations and variations with his left hand that it was too hard for us. Nothing could obscure the melody from him, but we were baffled. There was a polite, embarrassed silence.

'Can you play the tune alone,' asked SLO, 'to make it easier for us dullards, dear boy.'

RA was clearly very anxious. But he played it slowly and lyrically and gradually a very charming little waltz began to appear – the Sleeping Prince waltz.

'Bravo!' shouted Tony, and everyone began to applaud.

Then RA sang the song MM will be singing in the film, to another round of applause.

There is no doubt such a pretty tune could help the film immensely. David tells me there will be a grand ballroom scene with 500 people ('extras') waltzing to it in full evening dress. That is where the movie will differ from the play and hopefully be more of a spectacle.

After lunch I sneaked up to see my little Wdg* again – pretty

* i.e. Wardrobe girl.

as ever. She is no Einstein, but who cares about that. I just want to get my arms around her tiny waist and squeeze. She doesn't have a boyfriend, so I intend to make my move next weekend.

TUESDAY, 24 JULY

More arrivals from the USA. Most important is Paula Strasberg. SLO and Tony B have worked themselves into a lather about her already. She is MM's drama coach and current Svengali. SLO has been warned by Josh Logan (MM's last director on *Bus Stop*) that she is a total menace. She contradicted everything and she muddled MM up. I thought Lee Strasberg was the drama coach. I don't know what qualifications his wife has, except by association, although I hear she used to be an actress herself.

SLO has determined to ban Paula from the set while we are filming. Several times he has given me a diatribe about her and drama coaches in general. Finally, he told me to throw her out if I see her!

'She can stay in Marilyn's dressing room.'

'What about MM's dressing room in the studio?' (MM is to have her own sort of pre-fab, or 'portable' dressing room built for her right by the set. It too will be all decorated up in beige and soft lights.)

'Oh, the devil take her!' shouted SLO, seeing that he wasn't going to win.

Other arrivals from the USA are Amy and Joshua Greene, Milton's wife and baby son. Milton almost looks too young to be a father. He is evidently a famous photographer, although I hadn't heard of him. He does look a little like Bert Stern,* but that is hardly enough of a qualification. I will find an excuse to visit Tibbs tomorrow and meet everyone.

* A well-known New York photographer, married to Balanchine ballerina Allegra Kent.

There is also a lady called Rosten who used to work as AM's secretary and now is going to be MM's secretary.* She is said to be a chum of MM's but I suspect she is still loyal to AM. She will live with them both at Parkside.

WEDNESDAY, 25 JULY

I drove down to Tibbs in the morning – with Mr P's blessing. He loves a bit of spying, and I'm afraid he already sees the American and British camps as 'Them' and 'Us'. As I know Tibbs so well, and I was the one who arranged it, I went in through the back door as if I was the boss. This has a calming effect on the servants who are already in semi-revolt. It seems that Milton and his friends never give them a thought and are very untidy. The Cote-Preedys are definitely going to lose their staff if we are not careful. I persuaded everybody that the arrival of *Mrs* Milton Greene would change all the bad habits. They countered that by saying they had never been told there would be children.

'Just one,' I said, 'very small, and I have been told he is very well behaved.' (Absolute lie.)

But they may still walk out with no notice despite their huge wages. 'As good cooks go . . .'

Milton, to his credit, does not seem in the least surprised or upset when I wander into his living room unannounced.

'Hi Colin. Want a beer?'

I explained that I was just checking if he was comfortable and well looked after.

'Sure am. Stick around and meet Amy. She'll be down soon.'

Amy looks even younger than Milton. She is also extremely

---

* Hedda Rosten was the wife of Norman Rosten, a well-known New York novelist and poet. They both remained friends of MM all her life, and after her death Norman Rosten wrote a book about her entitled *Marilyn: A Very Personal Story*. He died in 1995.

attractive – small, pale, dark hair, intense – very much a contrast to my little Wdg with her empty eyes.

The little boy is about 2½ and known as Josh. He toddles all over the place, pretty much unhindered and with very little sense as yet. Milton seems very involved with both of them. Perhaps he is not as much of a rascal as Mr P implies. I absolutely can't help liking him.

In the afternoon I drove over to Parkside. Plod opened the front door cautiously (I don't know the staff here so I can't go round the back). It seems that MM and AM spend all their time upstairs, having meals and newspapers sent up. I met Hedda Rosten, MM's 'personal secretary'. She is very New York, middle-aged, but sympathetic and clever. She had a drink in her hand and seemed to me a little tipsy. I suppose she is still exhausted from the overnight flight.

Plod seems happy enough. It is a great relief to have him there.

As I was leaving AM appeared in a white towelling bathrobe and gazed round slowly over his hornrimmed specs. Plod explained who I was – the house etc. – but AM just grunted and went back upstairs.

And to think that this is the man the whole world envies – on honeymoon with Marilyn Monroe.

THURSDAY, 26 JULY

Mr P and I and Vanessa went to Pinewood again to check everything once more. (Vanessa is going to be Mr P's production secretary.) We already have Studio A and the major set – or scenery – is being put up there. It is going to be the purple drawing room in the Carpathian Embassy in Belgrave Square, and it is built so that each of the four walls, with their windows, fireplace, doors etc. can be swung away, and the camera can film the other three. There will be various bedrooms and dressing rooms leading off it which will be built later. It is meant to be on the first floor of the Embassy, and a huge columned hall and grand double staircase will eventually be put up in Studio B when we have finished in A.

There is a lighting grid or gantry all over the ceiling of each studio, with literally hundreds of lights hanging from it. They are on telescopic, rotating metal rods so that they can be altered by the electrician working up above. The lighting cameraman, Jack Cardiff, will work out which of these lights he wants lit, how high they should hang and where they should point. He will make a plan beforehand and give it to the lighting foreman, or 'gaffer', to set up. Then Jack will fine-tune all the lights using the stand-ins – one for MM, one for SLO, one for Dame Sybil Thorndike etc. until all is ready for the stars to walk in and perform.

The stars will be made up in their dressing rooms and walk in costume to the set. MM will do most of it in her main dressing room and then walk to her 'portable' dressing room for her costume. The idea is to have her ready to go in front of the camera at the same time as the set has been lit and prepared, and all the technicians are ready.

I get the strong impression that the technicians are the bosses here. If MM has to be kept waiting, so be it. Woe betide the actor or actress who keeps the technicians waiting!

That seems to be the attitude to British stars, anyway, but I doubt if MM will see it that way. Nor do I. There is no doubt that the technicians are admirable men – calm, professional, efficient. But basically they are replaceable and MM is not. Skills are common. Talent is rare. One day someone will have the courage to sack every technician in the industry and only rehire them if they promise to do what they are told.

However if I said that, even to David, I'd get lynched, so I better keep my mouth shut.

To go back to the filming – you never shoot a scene in one

Above: Marilyn Monroe and
Arthur Miller arrive at Heathrow,
escorted by my friends, the
policemen.

Right: Laurence Olivier
and Vivien Leigh greet MM and
AM at the airport (MM in
professional pose).

Below: Crowds of reporters force
MM and SLO to take refuge
behind a counter at Heathrow.

Left: MM with Donald Zec of the *Mirror*, shortly after arriving at Parkside House. Zec had just jumped out of the bushes, and MM had no idea who he was.

Below: AM, MM and SLO on arrival at Parkside House. My head can just be seen through the window behind SLO.

Above: Vivien Leigh and SLO in *The Sleeping Prince*, Phoenix Theatre, 1953. The dresses and uniforms were subtly changed for the film, and Vivien's character, 'Elsie Dagenham', became the more glamorous 'Elsie Marina'.

Roger Furse's original design for the salon, much changed for the actual filming.

MM at the start of filming.

Elaine Schreyck, Terence
Rattigan, an exasperated
SLO, an electrician and
Tony Bushell on the
'purple room' set.

Left: Richard Wattis,
Andrea Melandrinos,
SLO, Jack Cardiff and
Denys Coop.

Below: Dame Sybil
Thorndike, MM, Richard
Wattis. MM loved Dame
Sybil, but still couldn't
remember her lines.

go. You shoot all the bits with the camera pointing in one direction and then swirl round and shoot the others later. And each shot is done many times to get it just right. The boy with the clapperboard marks each one so that the editor can put the whole thing together in the right order later. The film goes off to a laboratory to be processed overnight. The sound is transferred from thin magnetic tape to wider tape in the Sound Department, and the editor uses the 'Clap' of the board to 'sync' the two up on his machine. The board also tells the production name, the shot number and the take number. The lab only prints the takes that look successful to the director – sometimes only one – in order to save money, but even so the editor ends up with hundreds of strips of film in his office, each one with a parallel piece of sound tape. I had asked David to explain all this and he took me round the studios showing me the various bits of equipment we would use. Cranes, dollies, B-P screens, arc lights, booms, concealed microphones etc!

I've got a lot to learn but David and Mr P have been very patient teachers. I really need to know as much as I possibly can before filming starts, so I don't get caught out.

The editor of the film will be Jack Harris. He is an old pro. Thin, grey hair, stoop and perpetual cigarette. At the moment he is finishing up another (British) film here, and normally he wouldn't join our production team until the actual filming was nearly over. An assistant would log all our footage, and sync it up for us to see in 'rushes' each evening.

But SLO (and Milton, I suspect) wants all the insurance he can get, so Jack H will start to work a week after filming starts in 10 days' time. Then he can double-check that every single thing has been covered by the camera.

David explained that with an 'inexperienced' (his word!) actress like MM,* there might be a little 'um' or 'er' or breath

---

* *The Prince and the Showgirl* was in fact her twenty-fifth film.

that the director didn't notice at the time. The editor will catch it on his machine – which he stops and starts while he examines every frame. Then they can either look for another 'take' or the director can shoot something to cover it.

This seems a good idea, especially as SLO will be acting in most shots as well as directing them. Tony B, bless him, could easily miss something. He's really not a professional director.

Jack Harris is as dour and thorough as Mr P – what politicians used to call 'a safe pair of hands'.

Pinewood again. Mr P was occupied with the accounts and legal departments of Rank Films who run Pinewood. They will rent us the necessary facilities. Very dull!

I spent the entire morning flirting with the little Wdg. Very exciting!

I finally bucked up courage to ask her for a date.

'Not tonight,' she said sternly.

'Why not?'

'I've got to wash my hair, of course.'

I didn't quite understand the 'of course', but pretty girls must be allowed their little ways.

'What about Saturday night then?'

'Oh, all right,' smile, giggle and wiggle.

She really has the smallest waist and the most enchanting laughing eyes I've ever seen. And all those beautiful natural (I suppose) brown ringlets hanging down to her shoulders. I'm hooked. I wish I could decide where to take her.

David and I checked the MM dressing room which had needed some alterations – not, I hasten to say, at MM's behest. I don't think she has even noticed where she is yet, but Milton feels he can interpret her wishes best. MM will use the suite to rest in from Monday, when rehearsals start.

We also checked the security arrangements. The idea is that no one can get in to our area unless they are on a casting call-sheet. For some of our scenes – the Coronation route, the Abbey, the ballroom – we will have as many as 500 'extras' and it would be very easy to smuggle a journalist in, so every-one will have to be especially careful. The 'extras' belong to a union – the FAA, or Film Artists' Association. It, too, is a completely closed shop – the film business seems full of them – and their members are the only ones who can do walk on parts in British films: passers by, crowds, people in shops etc. It is a small union so '500 extras' means using virtually all of them.

David says most of them, women as well as men, are total rogues. They all try to skive off rather than work, even though 'work' only means standing around in a costume. It will be our job to get them all in front of the camera, and keep them sober. We can be tough, but if we are not scrupulously fair they can all walk out on strike and stop the filming completely.

I met the chief security man at the gate. As I will be first to arrive each morning, I won't need a pass – but they will issue one anyway. I would imagine any reporter who did want to get in would be smarter than the Pinewood security men, and would have prepared a convincing story to fool them. But it would be tough to get past David.

I'm going to pick up my little Wdg at seven tomorrow night. She was very impressed that I have a car. Heavens, how ador-able. I haven't decided where to take her yet and I am a bit nervous. I have no idea what she expects.

SUNDAY, 29 JULY

What a super weekend. Not much to do with my film career, but all part of my film life, so I can't resist writing it down. The little Wdg is as sweet and tasty as a sugar mouse. I am head over heels with infatuation. I picked her up last night in the faithful Bristol. (I fear it has rather a musty leathery smell to it but she didn't seem to notice.) We went to Soho for dinner and I ordered champagne (!). She had one tiny glass and I nearly finished the rest. Lots of smarmy Italian service had a good effect. I didn't dare take her to a night-club. She might have been frightened by their dark, red, velvet corners. So we simply drove round the West End for an hour. She is very naive and all the sights were greeted with oohs and aahs. We chatted and held hands, where traffic allowed, across the hand-brake. Finally we came back here.* It is hard to invite anyone in for purely social reasons since I only have a kitchen and a bedroom, but we were both flushed with passion and fell onto the bed immediately. Her figure is picture perfect, she kisses like an angel (so I'm not the first) and she happily allowed me to stroke her all over.

Neither of us wanted to go the whole way. It is much too soon, and she is a good girl and not a tart. But it was impossible for her not to see how excited I was. She was curious, I explained, and finally out of kindness she put her little hand where the tension was and I was soon in heaven. Actually I think she enjoyed herself too, if not in quite the same explosive manner. When I took her home we were still delirious and spent ages kissing goodbye in the car. Finally a light came on in the house and she fled. Now I can't wait to see her again.

MONDAY, 30 JULY

Rehearsals at Pinewood all day. The principal cast members arrived at 9 a.m. David and I were outside to greet them and show them to an upstairs studio. It is just a large gloomy room with a few chairs scattered about, but David explained that to

---

* The servants' quarters of my parents' flat in the Albany, Piccadilly, which they had loaned to me. The flat is now owned by my brother Alan.

have rehearsals at all for a film is a great luxury. They are the essential preliminary of plays in the theatre, but evidently films very rarely have them.

MM will certainly never have had this sort of rehearsal before and I expect she was nervous. The normal procedure is to rehearse a scene 10 minutes before it is filmed. This is simply because an act of a play runs 45 minutes and a film shot lasts 45 seconds, more or less. I expect SLO has arranged for rehearsals on this occasion to ensure smooth, level performances right through the movie (a smooth level performance from Marilyn Monroe, to be precise). MM was only 45 minutes late, and was accompanied by Paula Strasberg.

Mrs Strasberg is not, at first glance, a very formidable figure. She is short and plump, with brown hair pulled back from a plain, round, expressive face. She has big brown eyes which are usually hidden by big dark glasses – like her protégée. Her clothes are also brown and beige – bohemian but expensive. Her influence over MM seems to be total. MM gazes at her continuously and defers to her at all times, as if she was a little Jewish Buddha. SLO was clearly put out by this, but remained theatrically gracious. He introduced MM to the assembled cast. First Dame Sybil, who radiates love and good fellowship so genuinely that even MM could not resist her. Then came Jeremy Spenser, who'll play Dame Sybil's grandson, very polite and bright-eyed, and Richard Wattis, who looks exactly like the Foreign Office dignitary which he will play. These three, together with MM and SLO, really *are* the movie.

Richard Wattis is in virtually every scene except the love scenes, and he even has to barge into two of those. Luckily he has a wonderful sense of humour behind his austere appearance.

Then SLO introduced Tony B, who had directed MM at the screen test, but whom MM had clearly forgotten, and then David and then me (two more blanks for MM).

Well, it has been 10 days since she saw any of us but frankly

I don't think she'd recognise Milton Greene in a crowd – especially if she was nervous. In this case she definitely was not at ease. The whole thing was rather theatrical and I sense that she doesn't understand the language.

All these people (except for David and me) are old cronies of SLO's. Paula understands them OK – she was once an actress herself – so she becomes MM's interpreter, and MM relies on her alone. SLO, whom I love and worship, can be a bit condescending. He treated MM like a doll from a faraway land. It is almost as if he is already in the character of the film, and she is just 'a little bit of fluff'. When SLO isn't completely at ease, he tends to retreat into a role, and in this case that is a little unfortunate. If MM is working with 'the greatest classical actor in the world' to acquire a serious dramatic image, then she won't be liking his attitude at all. Paula didn't say a word but she radiated disapproval, which definitely means that MM is upset.

Then SLO introduced the film. He told the whole story, most magically, and in a dozen accents, from start to finish. We really should have filmed his performance and then gone home. MM listened, eyes and mouth wide open like a child, completely carried away by the little fairy story. At the end everyone clapped and MM joined in enthusiastically. Then David and I handed round marked scripts and SLO chose certain key scenes to read aloud. I must say that MM was enchantingly unspoilt. Compared to those 'old stagers' she sounded most refreshing and delightful. But her voice does seem to be coming from another world, floating out of the sky like a little moth. I hope it all mixes together in the end. It *is* a fairy story, I suppose.

TUESDAY, 31 JULY

MM and Paula were 45 minutes late again today and it was enough to irritate SLO. He sees it as a great professional discourtesy, especially to Dame Sybil. This is a pity because Dame

Sybil really doesn't care, or hardly notices. I think MM actually enjoyed yesterday's readings and SLO should have taken advantage of this.

MM just doesn't seem to know late from early, so when she is scolded she often can't understand why – or is it that she doesn't want to understand why?

I took MM and Paula up to the rehearsal room where everyone was waiting. Dame S is so divine; she was warm and welcoming to MM – as if really glad to see her, as a human being. SLO tempered his greeting with a hint of menace which I could see MM pick up. Paula was icy to me but I am incredibly polite and charming to her at all times. As she does not know that I am in love with her daughter (sorry, little Wdg!) she was rather taken aback, but obviously flattered. MM, of course, totally ignores me, and quite right too. In the film industry I am right at the bottom and she is right at the top.

Actually she seems a strange mixture of self-centred and sensitive, like a child, I suppose. I have heard adults like that described as 'mimophants' – as fragile as mimosa about their own feelings, as tough as elephants about other people's.

I always thought being a big, big star would give you an armour-plated ego, but MM certainly has not got that. In fact I don't think SLO realises, or perhaps even cares, how fragile she is. He takes the line that all actors and actresses are nervous, but they should have learnt to suppress their nerves by the time they work with him. I hope he remembers that MM is his *partner* in this production – his equal business partner. Milton Greene is just his partner's stooge. Charming him won't help much!

I didn't stay for the rehearsals in the morning but went on the set with David. I've been on sets before and one thing hasn't changed. There is nowhere to sit! That's why directors and stars have their names on their chairs. The only place I know is the wheel of a sound boom, which is not popular with the sound boom operator. David thinks a 3rd Ast Dir should never sit, night or day, by definition. 'A 3rd Ast Dir is "he who never sits",' he barked.

I also had to pop up and see my little Wdg (sorry Susan!). Very sweet and soft and I stole a kiss behind the racks of costumes. The wardrobe mistress, her boss, has obviously been told the news of our night out together, and gives me looks which are both fierce and benevolent. 'Don't hurt my baby,' she implies.

I took a spare copy of the shooting script home, from rehearsals, and I'm going to study it very carefully tonight. Work before pleasure – but Saturday night seems far away.

WEDNESDAY, 1 AUGUST

MM was very late this morning. I phoned Plod to find out what was the matter but he knew nothing. Neither MM nor AM had come downstairs yet, and no one had had the courage to go up and knock.

'Could they have committed joint suicide?' I asked.

'No.' There had been bumps.

'What sort of bumps?' I heard Plod grin down the phone.

'Oh no. Surely not.'

I can't repeat *that* to SLO. He is extremely grim. It doesn't bode well for the 6.45 a.m. filming days. Tony B is fuming. Dear Tony, he always mirrors SLO so closely it is touching. He genuinely feels SLO's emotions as soon as SLO does. And his wife Anne is so like Vivien – in manner, of course, not in looks. Did he choose her like that, or did she become like that to please him?

The rest of the cast seem quite relieved. Esmond Knight paid us a visit – even though he is half-blind.* No one seems to

---

* Esmond Knight (1906–87) had been partially blinded in the Navy during the war. He acted in many films, including Olivier's *Henry V*, *Hamlet* and *Richard III*, and *The Red Shoes*. In *The Prince and the Showgirl* he played the Regent's security officer.

know how much he can or can't see, but he's very kind and nice.

Rehearsals went on, punctuated by hilarious theatrical jokes, mainly from Dicky Wattis. What a pity MM can't join in this sort of 'actors' band'. I'm sure it is much more relaxing than the method group in New York. But perhaps you have to be a professional, as these actors are, to be able to join in and relax.

At noon MM did turn up with Paula and Milton. I wonder if they are fighting over her. She seemed confused and frightened. The script might as well have been *Alice in Wonderland*.

She had trouble in following the other parts and so failed to come in when her cue came. No one could be cross; they were just embarrassed. Paula had gone off to 'confer' with Milton, so Dame S went and sat by MM and coaxed her through. I wish Dame S was going to be in every scene but she is only in about 15%. Something definitely seemed the matter with poor MM so perhaps it will pass. It could be her monthly period, I suppose, but she was clearly very upset. By the look in her eyes she has been taking tranquillisers. She went to lie down in her dressing room at lunchtime and Paula came tiptoeing out after a few minutes so she must have gone straight to sleep.

At 2.30, when she didn't appear, SLO told David and David told me to go to get her. Milton opened her dressing-room door, grinning, and said she'd be up in 10 minutes. I could see, and smell, a champagne bottle open on the table. My heart sank. I didn't mention what I'd seen to SLO. Not booze as well as pills?

Actually MM was much better in the afternoon. I suppose the tranqs had worn off and the champagne had cheered her up. SLO left her alone to do what she could and Paula sat silently in a corner glowering.

Milton must have won a round there, I guess!

THURSDAY, 2 AUGUST

MM arrived early, *for her*, at 10.30 a.m. Paula and Hedda Rosten and AM were with her in the car. (No room for Plod!) Tension seemed high to me but MM was quite jolly.

AM and Hedda just looked round the studios a bit and went back to Parkside. Paula took a firm grip of MM on one side and Milton, who had been waiting outside, took a firm grip of the other. They hardly bother to conceal their battle for control. And not just them – AM wants control too.

There is no doubt MM is a huge star. Everyone is simply hypnotised when she appears, including me. Everything revolves around her, whether she likes it or not, and yet she seems weak and vulnerable. If it is deliberate, it is incredibly skilful, but I think it is a completely natural gift. All the people round her want to control her, but they do so by trying to give her what they think she wants. What a paradox. Only Dame Sybil, with a heart as big as a house, can bypass all this nonsense. She can get away with being natural with MM because she is so naturally nice. Which none of the rest of us are, of course.

We are all really thinking of what we want underneath. 'Oh what a nice pot of gold you are. Can I help you, pot of gold?' etc. Dame S simply is not interested in gold.

Meanwhile life goes on. Filming starts on Monday and everything needs to be ready. Studio A is now bursting with technicians, preparing the equipment. The first shots on Monday will be unimportant – just there to make sure everything works, camera, lights, sound etc.

Jack Cardiff has to have the right lights hanging from the grid. It looks a total muddle but it has a pattern which only the gaffer and he understand. The lights get very hot – I dread to think what the temperature is up on the gantry. Whenever possible the lights are all switched off. 'Save the lights' is the cry, and there is a great clunk and what seems like darkness for a moment. But actually there are work lights which always stay on. They make everything look tawdry and pathetic. Carpenters are hammering, scene painters are finishing backdrops, curtains (drapes) are being hung and ornaments are being selected to decorate the set (props).

Roger Furse is meant to be in charge of the scenery but his assistants hardly seem to have time to listen to him.

Bumble Dawson is clearly close to a breakdown. She has all the costumes to worry about and some aren't to her liking.* My little Wdg, who works for Bumble of course, is too busy to give me anything but a smile, but we do have another date for Saturday night.

FRIDAY, 3 AUGUST

Tony B is incredibly nice. It seems he and Anne have rented a large house near Ascot, at Runnymede, where King John signed the Magna Carta. They want me to come to live with them there while filming is going on. It is much nearer the studios than London, of course, and not far from Tibbs and Englefield Green. Since I have to be at Pinewood by 6.40 a.m. every morning from now on, that is very good news.

But the real joy is to be invited to be part of 'the family'. Tony B and Anne are very much part of SLO and Vivien's 'family' and now I will be too. I always have a tendency to feel lonely unless I am with people. It is an absolutely lovely idea and I accepted with much gratitude.

Rehearsals ended at lunchtime and all the cast dashed off for the weekend.

'Not you,' said David sternly, and we stayed to see the last

---

* Some of the costumes had been designed by Cecil Beaton, but he had asked for too much money to do the whole production.

person leave. I don't mind. My mind is firmly fixed on tomorrow night.

I will go out to Tony and Anne at Runnymede on Sunday afternoon.

SUNDAY, 5 AUGUST

This is a glorious Edwardian mansion, with leaded windows, mahogany furniture and large Turkey rugs. The garden is very green and lush as we are near the river. The house is dark and cool. Anne is enchanting – slim, pretty, vivacious. She has filled the rooms with flowers and put the excess bric-a-brac in the attic. Tony is gruff and jovial. He brings generous drinks before dinner. I feel I have landed in Paradise! Anne cooked a delicious meal and the conversation sparkled.

My poor little Wdg is rather heavy going. Not a brain in that pretty little head. Anything that wouldn't go in a woman's magazine goes straight over it.

Lack of sophistication can be so attractive, and yet it's also rather tiring. Last night was delightful but I'm not sure that I can keep it going. What she likes is Romance. Well, I'm a great romantic, but she sees it only in terms of clichés. One step away from these simple terms and she is startled; one original remark and she gets suspicious. Alas, one cannot just kiss all evening. It might be different if we were sleeping together – then there is always something to do – but of *course* we are not.

Tomorrow we start to make a film.

The strain on SLO is going to be terrific. He has to direct as well as act. His confidence in his co-star and partner is minimal. Already late, already prone to be detached from reality, MM is the sort of star he just does not understand. It's no good treating her like 'a pretty little thing' who must do what she is told. When he does talk to her directly, she just gazes at him with those huge eyes, and it is impossible to tell whether she is even listening or not. I've never heard her reply. So SLO is forced to go through Milton, and he is sometimes forced to go through Paula. We must all be very careful not to take sides, or we will make things worse.

I feel as if this film has really become my life.

MONDAY, 6 AUGUST

I am officially 3rd Ast Dir at last.

'Your most important duty right now,' said David, at 9 a.m. in a crowded Studio A, 'is to get me a mug of tea and a piece of bread and dripping.'

We had all been there for over two hours by then, and we were very hungry indeed. A sort of NAAFI wagon appears in the concrete corridor at nine and my task is to queue for David's breakfast (and my own).

The studio is usually pretty dark except for the 'work lights', not to save electricity (money is no object in this film!) but to stop the set getting too hot. There is a real danger of the actors breaking out into a sweat – which is especially embarrassing if the action is set on a cold day.

Jack stands in the middle of each set, gazing at the stand-ins and giving orders to his 'gaffer'. Different lights are raised and lowered, switched on and off. Strange filters are added – 'barn doors' and 'gauzes' – and fingers are burned.

Except for the areas the cast acts in, the floor is completely covered with cables, camera rails and other hazards, so 'Have a nice trip?' becomes a much too frequent joke.

There are also a lot of people – electricians, camera assistants, boom operators, property men, make-up 'artists', wig-dressers, carpenters, drapery men, painters, plasterers, set decorators, etc., some of whom are busy, and a lot of whom are just milling around in case they are needed.

A journey from one side of the studio to the other with two mugs of scalding tea and two pieces of floppy 'Bread and Drip' is a truly hazardous experience. There must be at least 40 people in the way now, and I'm sure it will get worse when MM appears tomorrow.

The crew are all very English, very professional and clearly not easy to impress. They, of course, can see me for what I am – the lowest of the low.

There is Elaine, the continuity girl, whose job it is to make sure that every scene blends perfectly with its neighbours. Without her, cigarettes would suddenly lengthen or shorten, or jump from hand to hand, doors would suddenly open, and dresses rearrange themselves. Elaine is cool and competent and I get the impression that nothing will frustrate her.

There is Denys [Coop], the camera operator, and his crew. I didn't realise but Jack never even touches the camera. Very occasionally he is allowed to peek through it while everyone gives him odd looks. The camera is usually at the end of a long crane, or on rail tracks or both. Denys sits behind it, on a little chair with his legs either side, and twirls wheels to move the camera around. He also has two young men to push and steer, despite the use of electric motors. The sound recordist is Mitch, a very quiet, very patient man, who is often ignored by everyone. He has a metal console, linked to a microphone on a boom and to another recordist in a soundproof room somewhere.

Actually Mitch and this crew are more dangerous than they look, as they demonstrated while we were waiting this morning. Mitch saw Roger Furse and his assistant hobnobbing in a corner. A nod to his boom operator and the 'mike' was extended across all the obstacles until it was over Roger's head. Then a quick whisper to his recordist and the secret conversation was being played over the Tannoy system. Incredibly, even though their conversation was booming out from every loudspeaker, they didn't realise what was going on for over a minute. It could have been very embarrassing.

When we are ready to start filming David shouts 'QUIET, STUDIO. Going for a take. LOCK THE DOORS.'

A claxon goes PARP, PARP, PARP. Red lights flash. Denys says 'Camera rolling.' There are two little beeps from Mitch's console and Mitch says 'Speed.'

David says 'Mark it.' The clapper boy steps in front of the camera, names the film and the shot and the take number: '*The Prince and the Showgirl* (which is the new title) shot 3 take 1,' then he goes 'SNAP' with his clapper, on which the same information is written. Then the director – SLO or Tony – quietly says 'Action,' and filming starts.

This is essential for the editor. It gives him all the information on the sound tape *and* the film, so he can join the two up very easily. But it must be awfully off-putting for a nervous actor or actress. I suppose they have to learn to ignore it. It's all very well for the director to say 'Action' in soft and persuasive tones, but four other total strangers have just barked out their contributions, heedless of acting nerves.

As almost all scenes are very short, often just a few seconds, the director will be saying 'Cut' almost immediately and, nine times out of ten: 'Let's do it again.'

The happiest words you can hear are 'Print it' – you only print the very best takes – but even that is often followed by: 'Let's do it just once more, shall we, to be sure.'

Then Denys says 'Check the gate,' and his assistant opens the front of the camera and looks inside with a torch, to see that no fluff or 'film debris' has got caught on the shutter mechanism, and scratched the film.

All this is part of an inflexible routine. It happens every time a scene is filmed, no matter how often that scene is repeated. I can't understand how actors put up with it. Do they do the same in Hollywood? David says they do, but David's 'bark' alone is enough to frighten the lines right out of an actor's head. I suppose I will get used to it all, like any ritual.

Many of the people in the studio today were finishing up the set for tomorrow. The first set to be filmed – but not the first scene in the story of course – is the private drawing room of the Carpathian Embassy. SLO plays the Grand Duke, the Regent of Carpathia, and in this drawing room he will try to seduce the showgirl, Elsie Marina, MM. Also built is the Queen Dowager's sitting room, so that Dame Sybil's scenes can be shot as soon as possible.

The art director is a small intense lady with short grey hair, cut like a man's. She is Carmen Dillon, who has done many similar films. She works with a set dresser called Dario Simoni. Together with Roger Furse, they are responsible for the 'look' of the whole film. They are all completely professional, and only think about the scenery, and the props, and the costumes. They didn't even glance at MM when she walked in to look at the set for a moment last week, even though MM was quite excited by the whole thing.

This professionalism pervades the entire crew. In fact I am sure that they are all extremely proud of it. But I don't find it exactly 'welcoming' and I'm sure MM won't either. A top actor like Dicky Wattis will take it for granted. A director like SLO will insist on it, but a stranger, a foreigner, a 'new girl' like MM may be put off by it. I know I am. I admire and envy all their skills but it is possible to be human too, isn't it?

Anyway we did a couple of early shots which gave SLO and David a chance to get to know the crew before MM makes her very considerable presence felt. I had to stay until last so I only just got back here in time for Anne's dinner.

Tony B is buoyant for a change. This certainly means that SLO is optimistic, despite the omens. I expect he is happy to be working in a studio again, on a 'closed' set (no visitors) where Vivien's social demands have to take second place.

TUESDAY, 7 AUGUST

I left Runnymede at 6 a.m. sharp. Quite cool – no traffic on the road, so I was at Pinewood before 6.25. One sleepy guard who couldn't care less. After 20 minutes of pacing up and down outside the star dressing rooms, a black hire car arrived bearing ... Dame Sybil.

'Oh Colin. How kind of you to meet me. Dear me, you look cold.' (I was.) And she is over 70. I called make-up and hair and settled her in a warm dressing room. Five minutes later came Gilman in the Bentley, carrying SLO.

'Hello boy. Marilyn arrived yet?'

'Not yet, Sir Laurence.'

'Well wait here until she does and let me know directly.'

He is an optimist. At 7.05 Dicky Wattis arrived in a London taxi. With him was Paul Hardwick who will play the Embassy Major Domo. At 7.15, Milton Greene.

'Hi Colin. Is she here yet?' Who is he kidding? Then a long wait. I remain poised outside on the pavement. David emerged from the studios.

'What's going on? I thought you had a contact in her house. Have you phoned yet?'

'Not yet.'

'Phone.'

Plod answered. 'We are due to leave right now. We've been on standby for 10 minutes. Paula is here. She and Hedda are waiting too.'

Report to David. 'ETA, 8.15'.

Report to SLO (being made up) and Milton. 'ETA, 8.15.' Scowl.

At 8.30 MM arrives with Paula. Plod, carrying her bag, winks. MM wears dark glasses, beige nylon scarf, slacks.

'Good morning, Miss Monroe.'

'Oh, hi.'

Whitey is already in her dressing room. He has been there for nearly two hours. Everyone but Paula is firmly shut out. I report to SLO again.

Now I must make a note: 8.30 a.m. arrival at the studio means 11 a.m. on the set. It just isn't possible to hurry the Make-up – Hair – Costume sequence. Even if one could it might upset MM and then where would we be? Well, where? I expect we'll find out, sooner or later.

SLO had expected MM to be late and had planned 'cut-away' shots to use up the time.

The main scene of the day was Dame S – the Grand Duke's mother-in-law – greeting MM – the showgirl – in that purple drawing room. Jack had lit the stand-ins by 9 a.m. and by 9.30 Dame S and Dicky W were waiting on the set in full costume.

SLO offered profuse apologies but they didn't seem to mind.

'Poor dear. I expect she's nervous,' said Dame S.

'I expect so,' said Dicky dryly, but SLO did not get the point.

We shot a 'reaction' on Dicky, eyebrows up in mock surprise, and then I went to check on MM. As I was waiting outside her dressing-room door, she suddenly burst out, with Paula, Milton and Whitey surrounding her, like warders with a violent prisoner. They all swooped off in the wrong direction down the corridor, until I could run and catch up. When I got them into Studio A, they all bolted straight into the 'portable' dressing room on the set and slammed the door. This left Bumble, grinding her teeth and curling her lock of hair, MM's dresser (skinny, rather sexy), a hairdresser and a make-up assistant all marooned on the outside rather wondering what to do.

When they were eventually admitted it must have been like the 'And two hard-boiled eggs' scene from the Marx Bros.* The answer was to expel Paula and Milton but that is not so easy.

* In *Monkey Business* (1931).

Finally at 11.30 a.m., MM did emerge, fully dressed and looking, I am bound to say, ravishing. What a beautiful creature she is, to be sure. Paula whispered in her ear, and she walked straight on to the set.

No apologies to Dame S for a two-hour wait. But Dame S could see that it was quite an act of courage to be there at all and gave her a warm welcome.

'QUIET STUDIO. Going for a take. Hit the lights.'

The whole sequence began without SLO giving MM any direction, let alone MM asking for it. I suppose he just thought he would see what happened. He was sitting quietly behind the camera, in full costume as he was in the next shot.

'Action.'

Dame Sybil's performance is rock steady and flawless. All MM had to do was remember her lines.

When, by take 8, she had done this, we had a 'print' and MM's first shot was 'in the can'.

What a relief for us all, not least her.

Between takes MM cannot lie down, or even sit. Bumble's gorgeous dress does not allow for that. So MM has a strange white resting board with armrests on which she can relax. She dashes to this on every possible occasion, flicking her fingers up and down in the air. She has been taught this trick as a 'tension reliever' by one of the Strasbergs. It does not look very effective to me, and it gives her the appearance of being in a flap.

Paula's lips are never more than two inches from her ear, muttering and whispering continuously. Not unnaturally, SLO has a hard time coming to terms with this. He wants to talk to MM about the next shot, but it is hard for him to interrupt. I'm sure he had originally expected her to rush to him, and lap up his words of wisdom etc. Not a chance.

I hover equidistant from him and David while Jack re-lights as quickly as he can. During re-lighting, MM retreats to her mobile dressing room and once again the door is slammed. This time SLO knocked and walked in. Through the gap I could see a determined Paula trying to shield him from MM but he took no notice and shut the door behind him. David called 'the half' – union-ese for delaying lunch for half an hour – and we did another shot.

After lunch we did two more set-ups, and then David called 'That's a wrap, gentlemen,' signalling enough for the day.

We were all exhausted. MM got straight into her car with Whitey and Paula. Whitey will remove her make-up at Parkside and, I hope, calm her down. SLO and Milton retired to SLO's dressing room for 'a conference', and I could hear angry voices. I think SLO wants to nip 'this idiotic behaviour' in the bud. The trouble is that Milton does too, but he doesn't know how.

I went to the bar for a drink.

Thank goodness for Tony and Anne. I don't think I could have driven all the way back to London. I'm completely whacked. But I've sworn I will write this diary every night and that's going to be a good discipline.

WEDNESDAY, 8 AUGUST

Has anyone told MM that she's meant to be at the studios at 6.45 a.m.? Perhaps no one has dared? Perhaps it wouldn't make a scrap of difference?

I wonder what the usual time is in the USA. She turned up at 8.30 again this morning, quite jolly, and I even got a smile. But 8.30, early though it is in normal circumstances, is 1¾ hours late for us. Once again, we couldn't start filming with MM until 11.30. All the other actors have to be called for 9.00 on the set, just in case MM does turn up on time, and there are only so many shots we can shoot without her.

Lunch is almost due by 11.30 so David had to 'call the half' again. For some reason this annoys the crew. I know they are hungry but it's more than that. It is as if management was taking advantage of them in some way. 'Calling the half' is meant to be the exception, not the rule.

At least we all have time to explore the set and get to know each other. As usual I popped up to see my little Wdg. She is so pretty that I can't resist her, but she is also so silly that I jolly nearly can. I asked her for a date on Saturday.

'Of course,' she giggled. Of course. Already? Hmm.

Then I nearly brought the studio out on strike.

Dame Sybil was on the set in full costume and I asked her whether she would like to sit down.

'Why yes,' she said, 'let us all sit down,' so I went for her chair. Everyone froze.

'Are you a member of NATKE?' or some such bunch of union initials, asked some nameless man in overalls.

'No.'

'Chairs is Props. Props is NATKE. If ACT members (and I'm not even that yet) is going to do NATKE jobs, we're off.' They all grumbled and rumbled in agreement.

David stepped in to calm them down. 'Colin is a new boy,' etc., and put in a humble, official request for the chair for Dame Sybil, which took 10 minutes to fetch from the 'Prop' department (and should have been there from the beginning).

Now I know why it is so hard to sit down in a film studio! And they went on about what I had done all day. But Dame S is as bright as a lark, no matter what happens, and gossips away with Dicky W. They are a real theatrical pair.

The set is the drawing room on the first floor of the Embassy. Even allowing for the difference between Carpathian taste and mine, I find it completely hideous. Dreadful purples and mauves everywhere. But it is an effective background for the long white evening dress which MM will wear in every scene. I suppose Roger F was thinking of this when he designed it.

When MM is all made up by Whitey, in that sparkling outfit with her blonde wig, she really does shine like a star.

After we had done another four shots today (of the five that were planned – not so bad) we all went to see the film that had been printed from yesterday's material (the 'rushes').

It was only the best takes – two of each shot for comparison – but we were enraptured, all over again. The fluffs and the lapses of memory were forgotten. MM looked sublime and even acted old Dame S off the screen. She looks far more natural and less 'stagey'. SLO looked wooden and uncomfortable by comparison, although this is partly his role as Grand Duke. One can't tell anything about the film from one day's shooting, but one thing is for sure. You just can't take your eyes off MM.

SLO was still grim. I think he senses loss of control on many fronts. Well, he is nearly 50, poor man.

THURSDAY, 9 AUGUST

Now I know the secret of Paula's control over MM . . . total, abject sycophancy, continual flattery, blatant pandering to every nerve-end. 'Drama Coach' – phooey! It's Lee Strasberg who is the coach. But Paula certainly is an actress.

This morning Plod had reported serious insurrection among the staff at Parkside. I decided to go to talk to them, and to offer them a little more of MM's money, so at the end of the day I went back there in the front of MM's car. Plod had gone back at lunchtime. Of course I could have gone in my own car, but, to be honest, like everyone else in the world it seems, I couldn't resist getting more of MM's company. Anyway I don't think Paula minded. Nor did she notice that the glass division in the car was down.

As soon as we drove out of the studio gates she started: 'Marilyn, you were wonderful. You are the most wonderful actress I have ever known in my life, Marilyn. You are superb, Marilyn, you are divine.'

At this even MM demurred a little, and in truth she was not good today, having great trouble to remember even the simplest line. We had only completed two scenes.

Paula went straight on: 'Yes, Marilyn, you are a great, great actress. All my life, Marilyn, I have prayed for a great actress who I could help and guide. All my life, Marilyn, I have prayed on my knees.'

There was a bump and I sneaked a look. Paula was now on her knees on the carpet of the car.

'... prayed on my knees for God to give me a great actress. And now He has given me you, and you are that great actress, Marilyn. You are ...' all the way back to Parkside.

I was curled up with embarrassment, trying by sign language to get the chauffeur to put up the glass division, but he was much too stupid to notice – or to listen to what was going on. Paula was like a hypnotist on stage – you can't believe it will work, but it does. Gradually I could see MM relax, and regain the self-confidence which SLO and his gang had drained from her.

When we arrived I jumped out and opened the door. 'You really are great, Miss Monroe,' I said, and I meant it.

'Why thank you, Colin,' she said with a dazzling smile.

I didn't know that she'd noticed me, let alone remembered my name. I floated into the house and agreed to all the servants' demands – more money as I thought. I'll square Milton later.

The car took me on to Runnymede, still under MM's spell. But Tony and Anne brought me back to earth. After all, we have a long, complicated, expensive colour film to make somehow.

Tony will take me in to the studio tomorrow morning. If I am late, as he sometimes is, David can shout at him. No chance of MM beating me to it anyway.

FRIDAY, 10 AUGUST

Dame Sybil really is an angel. On time as usual this morning – she is now the only person who is – she handed me a bright red woolly scarf as she got out of the car.

'I thought you looked cold, so early in the morning, so I bought you this.'

I was overwhelmed. I'll wear it every morning from now on. Typical Dame S thoughtfulness. It is exactly what I need.

MM arrived at what is now her usual time. It seems there is nothing Plod, or Hedda Rosten, can do to get her out of the house before 8 a.m. I must say I sympathise. If I was the most famous film star in the world I wouldn't get up before nine. I know films don't work like that, and that if she is late it is phenomenally expensive, but couldn't she have asked SLO to schedule all her shots for after lunch? It would prevent a lot of friction.

As it is, he seems most upset by what he sees as MM's discourtesy to Dame S. This morning, through clenched teeth, he actually told MM to apologise to her. He strode onto the set when she arrived, took her by the hand as if he was dealing with a naughty schoolgirl, and led her over to Dame S. We didn't hear what he said but he had been rehearsing it for an hour. We all held our breath. SLO was doing what we were all dying to do, at last.

But MM wasn't at all upset – just surprised. I really don't think she realised that her lateness affected anyone. Plod says she gets called, goes back to sleep, gets called again, rushes round the house, changes clothes quite a few times, goes up and down stairs etc., without ever thinking of what the time is. Finally she bucks up her courage and dives into the car. Paula, Hedda, AM and Plod can all be flapping around her but it has no effect. Most of the time, and it is unpredictable, MM takes as much notice of other people as a cow does of rabbits in the same field.

However, Dame Sybil did get through: 'My dear you mustn't concern yourself,' she said. 'A great actress like you has other things on her mind, doesn't she?'

MM beamed, and behaved well all day.

We were only filming scenes with MM and Dame S, so SLO could stay behind the camera, and that makes things a lot easier. Then AM turned up to watch the 'rushes'. MM was thrilled, and giggled and wiggled like a teenager. When we got into the viewing theatre, to everyone's embarrassment they went into the back row and started snogging as if they were on a date!

'Love birds,' said Whitey with a grin, and we watched MM on the screen, endlessly repeating her lines, while the real-life MM heaved and panted a few rows behind us. Very un-British, but I suppose they are on their honeymoon. (MM's third, I guess.)

SUNDAY, 12 AUGUST

Saturday night was a bit of a failure. Oh, how quickly a beautiful bloom can fade. Already the little Wdg doesn't seem quite as charming as I thought, and not even as pretty. It is as if she belongs to the fringe – not really relevant, something I must leave behind.

Terry Rattigan is giving a party next Saturday night and I can *not* take the Wdg to it. Of course this is difficult to explain to her and in fact I can't even begin, so she has decided that I am going to take some other girl. The more I protested, the more she became convinced. Finally I told her, quite sharply, not to be silly. That caused a coolness which I fear may turn to ice. One problem is that she can never understand how I feel about my work. It really is so much more than just a job.

It's my whole life, and I'm afraid that she is right to feel excluded. But there is nothing I can do to change that.

Today Tony and Anne took me over to Notley for tea. Vivien was radiant. Without any doubt she is still the most beautiful woman in the world and she knows it. Terry Rattigan was there. He did not ask me to the famous party; but Vivien did, twice, in front of him, and anyway SLO had already done so on Friday. Also there were Roger Furse, Bumble and Bobby Helpmann.*

No one was there to represent the MM point of view so there were a lot of unflattering jokes about the Americans. Vivien was very funny and very catty and so was Bobby (well, he always is – even about Vivien).

Vivien, who knows I worship her, asked me confidentially how MM was working out. I dare not say anything or she might quote me, so I just rolled my eyes to heaven. Naturally she was delighted.

In the end we stayed much too late. Vivien hates to let good guests leave. It is already 11 p.m. and I have to be up at 5.45 as usual. Groan.

MONDAY, 13 AUGUST

We have now settled into a routine in that damn purple set. MM is late every morning and every morning it is treated with the same shock/horror/gloom by SLO and the entire crew.

SLO gets fully made up and costumed and the stand-ins are lit for the main scene. The equipment is checked and rechecked. We all eat bread and dripping and drink mugs of tea. Then we cast around for something to shoot – SLO speaks MM's lines to Dame S who has to pretend that MM is sitting opposite

* Robert Helpmann. Australian-born dancer, choreographer and actor (1909–86), knighted in 1968, who often partnered Margot Fonteyn. His film appearances included *Henry V* and *The Red Shoes*.

her. Finally MM appears, breathless and beautiful, and hope rises, only to be dashed as she disappears into her dressing room Mk II.

Fifteen minutes later – after goodness knows what little ritual – MM appears again and we all stand by. MM shakes her hands vigorously, one ear bent down to Paula (who is 10 inches shorter than her) for final encouragement.

If she gets panicky now it can mean another half hour in that portable Nissen hut, so Paula really is essential. MM might easily ruffle 'her' hair with one hand, and that means a 20-minute delay, or rub her eyes, half an hour. And SLO has yet to give her direction. Only he, after all, really knows what all the scenes are about, and he feels he must pass this on. Whether in fact he can say anything which has any effect whatsoever, I very much doubt. But he tries.

Then there is another hazard. Completely innocently, he may contradict something that Paula has just said. If she notices this, MM will summon Paula and Milton. Together they will go back through the corridor to the main dressing room and put through a long-distance call to Lee Strasberg in New York, usually waking him up. Advice from the great oracle.

Quite apart from the tremendous cost, in phone bills and Strasberg bills, this is hardly a vote of confidence for SLO. He is the director of the damn film, for heaven's sake, as he often points out angrily – to me and to Milton, but not to MM. And it doesn't help the action much, since Lee Strasberg is normally sleepy, and has absolutely no idea of what is going on over here (I don't think he even has a script).

When we do re-start, if SLO lets so much as a glimmer of his rage appear, a bright red flush suffuses MM's famous chest and neck which even Whitey cannot make disappear. Then filming has to stop for an hour while MM calms down and prepares to try again.

It's true that MM doesn't notice much of what is going on

around her, but the knowledge that 60 actors and technicians are waiting for you, and at enormous cost to you personally, is hardly one to induce calm in anyone, let alone someone with such a fragile grip on stability as MM. So there is a lot of handshaking and conferring, and finally she goes back to the main dressing room again to lie down. This in turn means that the dress must come off, and the wig must come off, so at least one and a half hours' delay is inevitable.

When we finally do get the shot, it is hardly as fresh as a daisy. SLO gets so tense that he can hardly act at all. Dame S stays as sweet as ever, but she loses that imperious edge that Martita Hunt* gave to the original role. Dame S is just too nice to be really royal. She has become like MM's dear old granny and this spills over into the part.

And yet, after all that grief, when we see the rushes it is *MM* who lights up the screen.

It is very bad luck on SLO. After rushes, he goes into his dressing room with Tony and Milton for yet more 'urgent discussions'. I see MM into her car and then go to the bar for a well-earned snort (brandy and water).

But this evening I had a hunch, and after half an hour I went back and started walking up and down outside the dressing rooms, while trying to look busy. Suddenly SLO stuck his head out, just as I guessed he might.

'Ah, Colin dear boy, could you pop over to the bar and get me some more cigarettes and a bottle of whisky?'

Well 'Colin' is determined to be the best damned 'gofer' in the movie world, so I opened the door of the empty dressing room next door, picked up the 100 Oliviers and the bottle of whisky I had left there, and marched straight in.

'Ah, thank you, dear boy,' said SLO, not bothering to question how I had got to the bar and back in 15 seconds. But

---

* (1900–69). British stage and screen actress, often cast in imperious roles (e.g. as Miss Havisham in David Lean's film of *Great Expectations*).

Milton jolly well noticed and he gave me a very quizzical look.

From now on I must stay within range, and prepared, until SLO has left the studio altogether.

I can't even gossip with Gilman outside in the car. One quick drink and then back on duty. I want SLO to think of me as *indispensable*, and take me on to his next production, as he does so many of his loyal crew.

I'm afraid this all made me late for Anne's delicious supper, but Tony understands without me telling him and he is big-hearted enough to be happy about it.

From now on dinner will be at eight and not 7.30.

TUESDAY, 14 AUGUST

To forget one's lines in midstream is evidently something no professional actor ever does. In a long play in the theatre it might just be forgiven once or twice. But in a film . . . ?!

Speeches in a film are usually very short. Four or five sentences must be the longest scene MM has to remember in the whole movie. Anyone watching a well-edited film won't notice the cuts and will think they have just seen one continuously acted scene.

MM doesn't really forget her lines. It is more as if she had never quite learnt them – as if they are pinned to her mental noticeboard so loosely that the slightest puff of wind will send them floating to the floor.

This is very disconcerting to the other actors. Like going down a familiar staircase and missing a step, MM is suddenly not there. She can be in mid-speech, and then she gives a little frown, her lips part, her eyes look puzzled, and she stops. She doesn't say 'Oh drat, what is the next line?' or anything. She just stops.

Sickening pauses are not permissible on film. SLO says 'Cut' quietly (and grimly), or sometimes 'Keep rolling' to camera and 'Would you like to try again?' to Marilyn. This has not yet been a success. Even if MM does have another try before the camera stops running, she is too flustered and her eyes are glazed.

Most actresses would take a quick peek at the script – which Elaine has, ready to hold out – say 'Oh yes. I'm so sorry. I know it now,' and have another try. They would only need a brief reminder to get it right. Not our MM. She walks off the set, leans on her recliner and waits to be powdered by Make-up and pandered to by Paula.

She's almost like an athlete taking a little rest before having another try at the high jump. And it may be that she feels that that *is* exactly what she is doing.

Dame S had a long line about Eleanora Duse being a much greater actress than Sarah Bernhardt. MM simply could not remember when to reply. Dame S is babbling on and ends with a rhetorical question: 'You agree. No?'

All MM had to say was 'No' at the right moment, but today even this proved too complicated. In the end we broke the shot down. We filmed the whole Dame S sequence, with MM missing out the 'No' altogether, and then filmed MM in close-up saying 'No?' which the editor will cut in later.

Halfway through, SLO tried a controlled explosion. MM was stunned, as usual, but SLO had reckoned without Dame S who promptly gave him a good ticking off.

'Don't you realise what a strain this poor girl is under? She hasn't had your years of experience. She is far from home in a strange country, trying to act in a strange part. Are you helping or bullying?' Poor SLO, who naturally thinks he is the injured party, was stunned.

MM was radiant.

'Oh thank you so much, Dame Sybil. But I mustn't forget my lines. I promise I'll try to remember them from now on.'

And she was good as gold for the rest of the afternoon.

Tony B thought this vastly amusing – 'Laurence got a scolding from Grandma,' he told Anne at dinner.

But SLO did not. 'It's high time someone gave that silly girl a real telling off,' he said to me, after Milton had left.

I worship SLO but I am afraid he is wrong.

WEDNESDAY, 15 AUGUST

I suppose you could say that today was a red-letter day. This morning I definitely saw more of MM than I ever expected to, and she went up in my estimation in more ways than one. She arrived really early, for her, and nearly caught us on the hop at 7.30 a.m. She was still in a jolly mood – I expect she and AM had had a good laugh over SLO's discomfiture.

As lunchtime drew near David caught me in the corridor, and told me to look for MM's marked script which was missing. I assumed this meant MM was on the set so I just barged into her dressing room and straight into the inner sanctum. What David had not told me was that filming had already ended.

There stood MM, completely nude, with only a white towel round her head.

I stopped dead. All I could see were beautiful white and pink curves. I must have gone as red as a beetroot. I couldn't even turn and rush out, so I just stood there and stared and stammered.

MM gave me her most innocent smile.

'Oh Colin,' she said. 'And you an old Etonian!'

How did she stay so cool? And how did she know which school I had gone to and what it meant?

When I managed to get out of the room and pull myself together, I realised that behind the fog MM could be a bit brighter than we all think. How much of the MM image is contrived? Acting dumb is a good way to make other people make fools of themselves. What fun it might have been to make a movie with MM when she felt everyone around was her friend.

Dream on, Colin.

In the afternoon we filmed Dame S putting her jewellery onto MM in preparation for her going to the Coronation, as Dame S's lady-in-waiting.

I don't know what happened at lunchtime – I hardly think it was my bursting in on her that did it – but MM had become really confused.

As Dame S and her original lady-in-waiting fuss round her, Elsie Marina has to ask 'What's happening? Is it a game?'

All light-hearted stuff, but by now MM was so frightened of missing her cue that she got frantic.

'What's happening?' she screamed in genuine distress. 'Is it a game?' like someone who is afraid they are being kidnapped.

No one could calm her down, so that's how it will go into the film. I hope it works.

We saw the 'rushes' of yesterday's footage, when her previous long scene with Dame S was broken down into three shots, and frankly I don't think that does work. When Jack lights a wide group shot he lights it quite differently from a close-up, especially MM. For the close-up he darkens the background and uses all sorts of filters to make MM look her best. That's fine, and MM does indeed look extremely beautiful, but it doesn't seem to match up with the wide shot which it will have to fit into. The wide shots look like a stage play, the close-ups are as intense as Garbo.

Yesterday MM had to look a little confused and say 'No?' It isn't hard for MM to look confused, so that worked fine. But today, when she looked very confused, it was almost too real for a light drawing-room comedy.

That is what this film is meant to be, and indeed that is what MM can often play so well.

SLO might have been able to handle this if he was left alone.

But everything has to bounce off Paula, and Paula always sees things in dramatic terms.

No wonder Jack Harris, the editor, haunts the studio like a gloomy vulture. He is going to have a tough job.

THURSDAY, 16 AUGUST

Nearly finished with Dame S – only three more shooting days. She starts in a stage play next week and is very tired. She is already in rehearsal, but she is still the only one to arrive on time (6.45) and we always have a little chat (she knows M and D of course). SLO's arrival is nearer to 7.15 these days and is always grim. Dicky Wattis and Paul Hardwick come tumbling in at the same time, but all the others use a different entrance.

Dicky and Paul have become my special chums. Paul plays the Major Domo, and has hardly any lines. This is a pity because he has a wonderful rich, dark baritone voice. I suppose this is his main asset as an actor. On this occasion it is wasted, but it certainly means that David has to 'sssh' him more than most when we are gossiping on the set. Dicky is always impeccably dressed in his Foreign Office uniform, with its gold braid and white stockings. He has a very 'camp' sense of humour, with lots of 'double entendres'. He is always ready with his lines, and never flustered by whatever MM does, or doesn't do. But he is so quintessentially British that she usually gazes at him as if he was from another planet. Dicky and SLO and Dame S can go through a scene like a knife through butter, and if MM is in the scene too, but doesn't have a line to remember, she quite enjoys herself, like a schoolgirl on a train. It is extraordinary that an actress can get so far without ever really being taught. MM just relies on her native savvy. Imagine what she would be like if she'd spent a year in rep. Or would the magic disappear?

Talking of magic, I now have a real problem with my little

Wdg. She is convinced that I am going to take someone else out this Saturday, and won't even let me explain. The atmosphere in the Wd department is so tense I can't even go in there. Wdg hides behind the racks of costumes, crying, while the wardrobe boss growls like a tigress. No sympathy from David when I explained the problem.

'The first lesson on any film production is not to shit on your own doorstep. Now you're stuck with this for another three months. I'm not having you unable to go up to Wardrobe for the rest of the film, so SORT IT OUT!'

What a nightmare. The trouble is that you can't discuss things logically with a little Wdg. I'll have to find the right cliché.

FRIDAY, 17 AUGUST

Dame S has left now and will be much missed. She had a calming, reassuring effect on MM, while SLO definitely puts the poor girl on edge. This morning MM had to eat a late supper, on screen. She had herself chosen caviar and chicken salad, but there were problems. It requires many 'takes' under hot lights to get a scene right, so fresh caviar and a new chicken salad were produced for each take. However there is a limit to the number of times that even the greatest actress can tuck into caviar and chicken salad at 11 in the morning.

I thought she did jolly well.

SLO kept telling her not to eat, 'just mime', but MM is now a '*method*' actress. She has to know what her motivation is for each action and each word, and miming does not come naturally to her. Nor did she appreciate the substitution of apple juice for champagne. Real champagne was produced, but it quickly got warm under the lights. By this time MM was supposed to have drunk lots of vodka (which was water of course) and she began to slurp on the real champagne a bit too greedily. SLO as the Grand Duke was on the telephone in the back of the set and couldn't see what was happening. Tony began to get nervous about continuity. How drunk was she meant to be? Soon Elaine, the continuity girl, was beginning to direct the movie. MM liked this but the rest of the crew did not.

SLO sensed impending chaos and got frantic, huffing and puffing away from the far corner.

MM was enjoying herself. She also had a chance to be patriotic about America and raised her glass to toast 'the President' (Taft), which was an action she found profoundly sympathetic to her mood. I'm sure she feels that the British treat Americans as if they were idiots every bit as much as the Carpathians did in 1911. As MM got more confident, SLO began to fade, very rare for him. It is hard to believe that even a Carpathian Grand Duke would be quite so wooden to a young lady he is hoping to go to bed with in half an hour.

In the afternoon, Jeremy Spenser* appeared for his first entrance. He looks 16 but I suppose he is about 22. I recognise him from somewhere. Did he play Sabu, the elephant boy?** It's the sort of question that is hard to ask.

In this part his carefully contrived royal charm, flicked on and off as if by a switch, is more convincing than SLO's, and he is equally smooth off-screen. MM seems to like him but perhaps it is also because his character in the script is so sympathetic to hers.

It is clear that she does sometimes have difficulty separating fact from fiction, as many actresses do. Vivien, after all, has never quite escaped from Scarlett O'Hara. In the *Sleeping Prince* story, SLO plays an insensitive seducer, and MM must have come across a great many of those in her early career. In real

* Former child star, b.1937. He was playing the part of Nicky, the young King.
** In fact the title role in *Elephant Boy* (1937) was played by the *actor* Sabu (Sabu Dastagir, 1924–63).

life, he plays an insensitive director, and she has come across those before too. It is not a happy combination.

And we still have to get through the love scenes!

SUNDAY, 19 AUGUST

Terry Rattigan's party last night was as formal and artificial as his plays.

He has a typical expensive show-business house on Wentworth golf course – 1920s classical, and very nouveau riche; thick carpets, chandeliers, flowers.

I got there early, and alone, and the first person I saw was Mr P. I got a shock as it was the only time I'd ever seen him not in his brown suit. He was wearing an old-fashioned dinner jacket, and a wing collar, but at least he still had his pipe and hornrim specs. With him was Mrs P. She is just as conventional as he is, and clearly very proud of her old stick of a husband. Perfect casting!

Terry R was in a white dinner jacket beaming urbanely at everyone (though not me).

Milton was there with Amy – small and attractive, both of them. Finally AM and MM. AM looked very dashing, also in a white dinner jacket – strong jaw, intense gaze, the perfect he-man intellectual. I fancy he is very vain indeed.

MM looked a bit straggly. She had done her hair herself and she had not been made up by Whitey. She even seemed a bit scared, not of us, but of AM. He really is unpleasant. He struts around as if MM were his property. He seems to think his superior intelligence puts him on a higher plane, and treats her as if she is just an accessory. Poor MM. Another insensitive male in her life is the last thing she needs. I can't see the romance lasting long. She is the one who could be forgiven a little vanity but, strangely enough, that's not in her make-up at all.

I hung around SLO in case I could be of help, but he was soon surrounded by people of greater assumed self-importance, mainly agents.

Cecil Tennant treats me like an office boy, which I am I suppose. He is married to a Russian ballerina* and even she is not very friendly, which is a surprise. All the ballerinas I've ever met are adorable. Karsavina,** who we once met in Hampstead, was as lovely as Margot, although very old.

The party just never gelled. I bet it would have been another matter if we were all queer. (Gaiety, everyone!) I left early and went up to London. I went to the Stork Club and in the end I was unfaithful to the Wdg – so she was right!

MONDAY, 20 AUGUST

A bad start to the week. MM did not show up until 11 a.m. Frantic phone calls to Plod at Parkside were to no avail, although he did hint darkly that AM and MM were not on such friendly terms as usual. I thought so on Saturday at the party.

I reported this to SLO. He said that AM is short of funds, and has finally figured out that when MM is late at the studio, she loses money. And when MM loses money, he does not exactly get richer. Like many American intellectuals he is extremely mean – or maybe meanness goes with vanity, like Garrett Moore. In any case he has been trying to get MM out of the house earlier in the mornings.

I suspect he also wants peace and quiet. I certainly wouldn't want a frantic MM in my bedroom all morning, unless of course we were 'playing trains' in Plod's immortal words. Now, it seems, AM has lost some of his powers of persuasion. Nobody knows, or will say, what the trouble really is.

We did all the shots of SLO and Jeremy which MM isn't in,

---

* Irina Baronova, star of the de Basil Ballet in the 1930s.
** Original Prima Ballerina of the Diaghaleff company, partner of Nijinsky.

but we couldn't work with her until after lunch. When we did it was a long scene and not all that easy. She comes in through the door of the purple room with Dicky W and says, 'Oh, we are the first to arrive, aren't we?'

Then there is a change of thought, which is always tough for MM unless very carefully explained by one (and only one) person. She looks round the opulent room and is supposed to say: 'Gee, this is all right too, isn't it.'

Alas, it was not carefully explained (and never by one person) until after tempers had already begun to fray (about take 5). In she came each time:

'Oh, we are the first to arrive, aren't we?' Fine so far.

'Gee, this is all right, isn't it?'

'CUT.'

'Wonderful, Marilyn darling, but the line is "Gee this is all right TOO, isn't it?".'

Much conferring. Much 'Oh yeah, gee, I guess so,' much leaning, flicking of fingers, whispers from Paula, powder re-applied, wig patted, dress straightened and off we go again.

David shouts: 'Going for a take. Absolute QUIET please.'

The lights come on with a crash. Bells ring, doors lock with a clunk, red lights flash.

'Camera running.'

'Sound.' Beep, beep.

'Speed.'

'Mark it.'

'*Prince and the Showgirl* shot 48 take 6.' SNAP.

'Action.'

MM and Dicky come through the doors.

'Oh, we are the first to arrive, aren't we?'

We hold our breath. MM looks round.

'Gee this is all right, isn't it.'

'CUT!' etc. etc.

In the end it was Dicky who explained to her that in an

earlier scene, not yet filmed, she had come in to the hall of the Embassy and said 'Gee, this is all right.' That is why it was now so important to say 'Gee, this is all right too!'

Finally she got it right and carried on to the end of the scene without a hitch, but what a painful hour it took.

Like a Greek tragedy, it really isn't anyone's fault. SLO would normally take his leading lady quietly to one side and explain it after the first mistake. But MM is all revved up by Paula, before each scene, to go it alone. And after she makes a mistake, which in this case Paula probably didn't even notice, it is Paula and not her director to whom she runs. When the wretched director does intervene, simply to get his film back on the rails, MM is already upset, and it is hard to talk to her on any level.

What is so frustrating is that we all know that in the end only the good take will be printed, and tomorrow evening MM will fly out of the rushes like an angel.

At this rate the film will take forever. I don't know why we are all so fed up with that purple room set but we are. It is cut in half, and sometimes in quarters, so that the camera can shoot in different directions, across the table, above the sofa, looking at the fireplace, or the windows or the door. But it always feels claustrophobic. I expect it is the colour. The whole crew feels the same. Only Dicky's camp, unprintable comments break the tension.

TUESDAY, 21 AUGUST

Whenever something goes wrong in the studio during filming, the blame either falls on MM or on some technical mystery. But today I think the blame fell on the doors – those doors into the purple room through which everyone has to enter. Mind you I'm not sure if SLO or Tony or David would agree.

In the opening shot of the day, MM was due to burst in

through these doors and surprise Dicky and SLO. She had been
'below stairs' with Nicky, the young King, and the Grand Duke
has only just been told that she is still in the Embassy. He is
expecting an old flame, Lady Sunningdale, to come to supper.
Lady Sunningdale is late and he says he wishes she had grown
out of that habit. His line is: 'She has had, after all, time,' and
that was MM's cue. Her line is: 'Hello. Oh – supper! How
thoughtful of you, darling. I'll just run down and say goodnight
to Nicky. See you in a minute.' Then exit. Not too hard for her
– all one 'thought'.

David shouts: 'Let's go for a take. QUIET studio.' MM is
tucked into a little bit of corridor outside the doors, where she
can hear SLO's cue. We go through the ritual as usual. Lights,
Camera, Sound etc. 'Action.'

SLO: 'She has had, after all, time.'

Nothing. The doors do not move an inch. No sound. No
clues. Nothing.

'CUT.' Controlled passion now from Tony.

'Marilyn? Is anything the matter behind there?' Muffled
grunts.

'COLIN!' Would you go behind those doors and see if you
can help Miss Monroe!' I dash round the corners of the set
(quite a long way, as it happens) to find MM smiling mildly in
her little alcove. She seems as mystified as everyone else.

'Any problems, Miss Monroe?' She shakes her head with
wide eyes.

I am not empowered to say 'Well, what the hell is going on
then?' so I squeeze into the little alcove with her and wait.

'Going for a take, studio?' I hear distantly.

'Lights.'

'Camera.'

'Sound.'

'Action.'

SLO: 'She has had, after all, time.'

I am holding the handle of the door, and I pull it firmly towards me, so that MM can burst in with her line. Nothing. The door doesn't budge. Then and only then do I remember that the doors open inward and not out into the corridor. Too late. There is a bellow of rage simultaneously from Tony, David and SLO. 'COLIN!'

I caught MM's eye and we both dissolved into total, helpless giggles. The more they cursed from the other side of those nice strong doors, the more we laughed. The tears literally ran down our cheeks and we were both incapable of speech. David marched across the set and flung open the doors to expose us to the whole studio, helpless as naughty school children. MM buried her face in her hands and rushed off to Make-up for half an hour – plenty of time for me to get an old-fashioned roasting from David and Tony. I couldn't really explain, and nobody in the whole studio thought it was funny – except for Marilyn and me. She really can be adorable when she is human like that.

Tony was very gruff at dinner tonight, but Anne thought it hilarious. How like a married couple.

WEDNESDAY, 22 AUGUST

'Vivien is coming to pay us a visit today,' said SLO when he arrived this morning. 'Call me when Marilyn gets here. I'd better butter her up a bit first.'

Gilman gave me a wicked grin. Vivien is famous for being unbelievably catty while at the same time being unbelievably charming. I did not think Vivien's visit was a good idea, under the circumstances, but of course no one can stop Vivien doing something if she has a mind to it. It was Vivien who created MM's role on stage, and MM knows this well. I suppose Vivien would have liked to do the movie herself too. 'But Larry went and fell in love with Marilyn, silly boy,' she said to me at

Notley: 'And a fat lot of good that did him.' (Vivien is *always* right.)

I suggested caution to SLO, but he had a mischievous look in his eye. Perhaps he thought Vivien might inspire MM to greater efforts.

Vivien arrived at lunchtime, after we had endured another painful session in the purple room. SLO, in full costume, escorted her on to the set as if she were royalty.

'Hello, Colin darling' – that got the crew's attention – 'Are you looking after Larry for me like you promised?'

Me: 'Gulp.'

Tony: 'We are all trying our best, Vivien.'

Vivien advanced and, to MM's intense surprise, kissed her lightly on both cheeks.

'Marilyn,' she sighed, 'Larry tells me you are quite, quite superb. He never stops singing your praises. I'm getting a little jealous.'

Very sweet, very sincere, what an actress! MM smiled and fluttered her eyelids, easily flattered although not quite convinced. Since Vivien was looking stunning in a little Jacques Fath suit and MM was looking like a plump frump in a towelling robe, the crew could hardly imagine Vivien being jealous. But still, it was a true meeting of the stars. Everyone was impressed, even Paula. Vivien quickly made her excuses.

'I know how frantically hard Larry makes you all work etc.,' and she vanished in a cloud of very expensive perfume. Even David, who has bellowed at every film star in Britain, was in a bit of a dream.

MM took a long time to emerge in the afternoon, but she did definitely seem more committed and we got a surprising amount done. Tomorrow we do the love stuff on the armchair. Fingers crossed.

THURSDAY, 23 AUGUST

I have been watching MM very closely. She is really like a lovely child. Whatever possessed her to become an actress? I suppose it was some sort of clichéd idea about Hollywood. In America pretty blondes with buxom figures often think that they are meant to be film stars. Or perhaps it was some man who found that the quickest way into her pants was to promise that he could get her into movies. MM is certainly very ambitious. Once she got to LA,* I'm sure she found a whole string of men who told her that they could get her into the movies, and she must have been very single-minded to get where she has. Many pretty girls are convinced that they are 'someone special', and she was proved right!

A natural on camera MM certainly is, but a great actress she is not. When SLO, or Dicky or Dame Sybil act, they stop being who they are and become the character who they are acting. They enjoy changing into someone else completely. It feels natural to them, often better than real life. They can become heroes, villains, lunatics, poets etc. depending on the script they are given.

With the minor actors on the set it may be different. Take the footmen, for example. One or two may be burning with ambition. They will be acting footmen with all their might – dreaming of the day when they will be acting the Grand Duke. The other two may be earning their living the easiest way they can, and just walking where they are told to, without a thought in their heads.

MM is different again. She desperately wants to be an 'actress'. She has been told many times, by the people who see her magic in front of the camera, and also by unscrupulous

* In fact she was brought up in Los Angeles.

people who just want her money, that she is a wonderful '*actress*'. She is not. MM is always MM. Can one imagine her playing a ruthless spy? Most of the time she is desperately trying to remember her lines and the 'motivation' of the character who speaks them. This automatically precludes 'being' the character. The *character* doesn't have to think of lines and motivation. So the process of acting is very frightening for her. She needs Paula a few feet away and Lee at the end of a phone to reassure her. But there is no easy formula, no short cut. I suspect that there have been quite a few 'Paulas' in the past, and all of them will ultimately fail because they are substitutes for a training which is just not there.

FRIDAY, 24 AUGUST

MM's scenes are made even harder by the idiotic Rattigan script. In the middle of her first love scene, after the Grand Duke has finally kissed her on the sofa, she is supposed to run her fingers through his hair. Well this is very difficult and unpleasant because SLO's hair is greased absolutely flat, but would she really ask him what he used on it? She's not a beautician. But this is what the script would have her do.

'Oh, a little pomade,' the Grand Duke replies abstractedly, and she is meant to reply 'You should use Pinaud's "Lilac".'

What on earth is this interchange doing in the love scene between Marilyn Monroe and Laurence Olivier? It's hardly the place for a witty quip, or a laugh for that matter.

It was far too much for MM to remember – no 'motivation' at all. She plunged in bravely, forgot, desperately tried to remember after all, and finally blurted out: 'You should use' – loud squeak – 'I know, er, er, er PINAUD'S "LILAC"' giggle giggle. SLO, his face two inches from hers and due to kiss her passionately in the next shot, was trying frantically to cover the gaps and keep a straight face.

'Think of love, my darling,' he gabbled. 'Don't forget our *love*.'

After many attempts, he decided to print everything and choose the best one. Everyone hopes it will work, but it may look a little odd, to say the least. Perhaps it will be a triumph of nature over art.

It has been a tough week. SLO and Milton are shattered. So is AM. He came over to collect MM but ended up sending her on ahead with Paula and Whitey and Plod. I went into SLO's dressing room with fresh whisky and cigarettes.

'I've had it,' said SLO. 'I think I'll go off to China for a month.'

'I'll come with you,' said Milton, laughing.

'So will I,' said AM grimly.

'Come now, dear boy,' said SLO. 'Your new bride.'

'She's devouring me,' I heard AM say as I left.

Three strong, famous men all in awe of that young lady. Luckily they take no notice of me whatsoever, which I *think* is a compliment.

Before I left the studio, Plod rang from Parkside. MM had announced that she wants to go shopping tomorrow – incognito. Plod is nervous and wants me there too. Parkside at 10 a.m. But no one is to tell Milton. I went and told Milton right away and then came back here for supper.

SATURDAY, 25 AUGUST

I arrived at Parkside at 9.45 a.m. Milton was already there.

'Colin. What's the smartest shopping street in London?'

'Bond Street.'

'OK. We'll go there.'

Plod went off to make a discreet phone call (to Gerald Row Police Station I expect) and Milton and I sat and waited ... for one and a half hours. Milton is a great charmer, very easy-going and direct. He told me he used to be a top photographer which is how he got to meet MM.* He genuinely feels that MM was being exploited by 20th Century Fox – nothing new about that – and he wanted to help her escape from her contract. And that I can understand too. Everyone who meets MM wants to help her, even me. It is another part of her magic. Milton teamed up with a lawyer called Irving Stein who Milton said is as brilliant as he is unsympathetic. (The 'unsympathetic' bit is right. I 'met' him when MM first arrived.) Together they succeeded in getting MM free and Milton set up Marilyn Monroe Productions. But he underestimated the power that MM generates, and the number of people who are determined to get a piece of that power. Trying to control MM is like riding a tiger. With the best will in the world, you can't really control, or even forecast, which way it is going to go. So Milton is forever trying to *manipulate* MM with promises, threats, even drugs** – and he has to compete with Paula, AM, Hedda Rosten, various psychiatrists and doctors and, ultimately, SLO and me. I feel sorry for Milton. He wants to get the film made as much as we do, and he has a very difficult job, as pig in the middle.

When MM did come down at 11.30 she was in a sulky mood. She was all in beige as usual – tight blouse, slacks, head scarf – and dark glasses, with very little make-up. She looked like she had when she first turned up at the studio. She was not in the least surprised to see Milton, or me. AM and MM and Milton and Plod got into the Princess and I followed in the Bristol. When we got to Bond Street, I could immediately see a problem. We were late, as usual, and all the shops were going to shut at 12.30 (Saturday early closing). Nobody else in the party seemed to mind, however, so we all got out and trooped along behind AM and MM. As AM is pretty tall and MM is pretty wiggly, we expected quite a reaction, but no one seemed to

* They had had a brief affair in 1949.
** Though never hard drugs.

notice. The most famous couple in the world (bar two, I suppose*) were strolling along a busy street with no protection, and nothing happened.

All of a sudden Milton realised that MM was *not* happy about this. She wanted to be incognito, but she didn't want to be *that* incognito. Not mobbed, perhaps, but a round of applause might have been nice! But the shops were now shutting and the crowds were thinning out.

'Where are the big shops, Colin? Where is everybody?'

I wheeled the party into Regent Street. I could see a few policemen around, winking at Plod, so I felt reassured. Then suddenly we were surrounded. I don't know who spread the word, the police or Milton, or perhaps some reporter Milton had called earlier. The crowds picked up the scent of a 'star' and it took all Plod's chums to help us fight our way back to the cars. For the first time I saw how dangerous a leaderless mob can be, although in this case they were driven only by curiosity. Poor MM was quite upset and shaking, despite AM's arm round her. But perhaps she is used to this sort of horror, and even welcomes it, to confirm her view of the awfulness of her life. AM had also had quite a fright, though nothing really shakes his air of smug complacency. He is much more pleased with himself than MM is with herself, that's for sure. Plod worships MM, and can't stand AM, and nor can I. (And to be honest, we are probably a little bit jealous too!)

MONDAY, 27 AUGUST

No MM today. Calls to Plod yielded no clues, and at lunchtime we gave up hope. Finally AM called to say that MM wasn't well. A fever. Hmm. We had some shots we could do with SLO, Paul and Dicky. We also have prepared the corridor

---

* The other two couples I had in mind were Jacqueline and John F. Kennedy, and Prince Rainier and Princess Grace (Grace Kelly).

outside the purple room for shots of the valet and the other staff playing music in case MM doesn't come tomorrow.

When MM isn't on the set, SLO is a different man – tough, direct, clear-minded. Filming goes like clockwork, of course, because the other actors know him so well. But we all seem to feel that the centre of the film is missing, that what we are doing is peripheral. It's almost too easy. MM is so difficult to work with that even hardened technicians are driven crazy. But when she doesn't show up, we miss her! What a paradox. All of a sudden, filming is so routine that there is nothing to write about.

TUESDAY, 28 AUGUST

Despite our fears, MM did show up this morning, and at 8.30, but she didn't look well. I reported as much to SLO in his dressing room. A lot of people see each of them as soon as they arrive, but I'm the only one who sees them both.

'What shall we do, Colin?' he said wearily. 'What can we do?'

'Can we switch to something simple? It's that or nothing, I fear.'

'OK, send Jack (Cardiff) along. And Elaine (Continuity). We've got time to change things around.'

I explained the situation to Jack, and to David. Jack went to see MM for himself, but came out after a few minutes.

'I think she's drugged,' he said to SLO. They looked at the shot list to find something easy which we could use in the only set which was already built and lit. Luckily there were two shots of MM in close-up, lying on the floor. Jack went off and spent an hour with MM's stand-in and the lighting crew. At this stage in the film, MM is supposed to have drunk too much vodka and passed out just as the Grand Duke is about to seduce her. So all she had to do this morning was to lie back and giggle 'Oh, look at those lovely cherubs on the ceiling,' and 'Good night, my darling. See you in the morning.'

Even in her woozy state, MM managed to do this quite quickly, so after lunch we filmed her and SLO on the sofa. By now she was so relaxed that she was actually very funny. Dicky W has to burst in and interrupt SLO and MM in a clinch. He has an alibi that MM no longer needs.

'Your aunt has been in a serious motor accident, Miss Marina.'

'Oh, go away you silly man,' giggled MM. 'Serve her right. She shouldn't be out at this time of night. She's 93!' More giggles. Suddenly she really was *acting*. And for a moment we forgave her everything.

WEDNESDAY, 29 AUGUST

MM was very late this morning. Paula was tense and Milton was even tenser. Plod told me that MM and AM had a row in the night, and AM could not control MM at all. She was wandering around the house in a very distressed state. There had been a lot of phone calls, many of them transatlantic. Finally Milton had gone over with extra pills. MM had called for Whitey Snyder, but of course he is long gone. In the end one of the doctors in New York talked to her until she was calm enough to go to sleep. (Imagine what *that* cost!) AM had completely washed his hands of her, and Paula, usually her best friend and sort of surrogate mum, couldn't help on this occasion. Although Paula does want to control MM as an actress, she genuinely does not want to get between MM and AM.

We managed one long-shot of MM warning the Grand Duke that he'd better watch out because she is falling in love with him – just before she passes out.

SLO had to murmur 'Oh my darling, my beloved' or some such nonsense just to keep her going, and this did seem to test

his acting skills to the limit. MM was in another world – quite
cheerful but ga-ga. Booze *and* drugs I suspect. Nothing seemed
to get through to her. But she is meant to be drunk in that
scene, so I expect it will look wonderful, as usual. At least the
scene is 'in the can'. When MM went back to her dressing
room, it was clear she wouldn't be back on the set again, even
though she didn't leave the studio.

We did reaction shots on SLO but our troubles weren't over.
A piece of painted ceiling to go over SLO's head – referred to
by MM yesterday – 'Oh what pretty cherubs . . .' – was not
ready and there was a great row. Teddy, Roger and even
Carmen were all in a flap. I think it was partly the aftermath
of the tension with MM. When she is so removed from the
everyday world we live in, it is very hard to keep patience. The
whole studio gets 'on edge'. One thing is certain, however. If
you scream at her or even frown, she retreats further into her
unreal world, and gets even harder to reach. SLO calls it the
Ophelia Complex. We don't expect her in tomorrow.

THURSDAY, 30 AUGUST

AM went off to Paris today, which may explain why MM was
in such bad shape yesterday. Rumour has it that he is going
back to NYC after Paris and will be away for over 10 days.
AM seems big-headed, insensitive and super-selfish. I never
saw him look tenderly at MM, only with what looks like a
sort of boasting self-satisfaction. What bad luck on MM. Why
couldn't she have found what she really needs – someone sympathetic to support her? She doesn't move around with those
sort of people I suppose.

We've finished all the 'cut-away' shots we can in the purple
room. We will do the Grand Duke's dressing room next, and
then we will move on to the hall and staircase.

In the meantime, we have scheduled a day on the lot for

tomorrow. We have ordered all the 'extras' available – about 500 – from the FAA. The costumes are already prepared, which means a lot of visits to the wardrobe department. The atmosphere up there is arctic, but, alas, there is nothing I can do. It is over. Poor little Wdg. She'll probably be married in a couple of years. Two kids and a family car. Wdg heaven!

Milton spent a long time with SLO and they decided to give MM a day off tomorrow. Then she can have a long weekend to rest in. She doesn't claim to be ill, but there is definitely more than one problem on her mind. Perhaps with AM gone, she'll get a chance to work quietly on the script with Paula. A lot of film stars first look at the day's lines while they are being made up – as MM does – but no other actor on this film does that. SLO expects them to know the whole script by heart before they arrive, like in a play.

FRIDAY, 31 AUGUST

500 extras are a hell of a handful. Just as David warned, they go to amazing lengths to avoid working. They also make desperate efforts to get paid double and the combination of both these pressures is bizarre. If they are in a medium shot with a principal actor, what they call 'cameo', they get more. If they have any special responsibility – whistling, juggling, grinning, they get more. If they wear any item of their own clothing, they get more etc. They are each issued with a pay slip and it is up to the assistant directors to add on bonus items. We also have to sign each slip before they can get paid at all. Our ultimate threat is to sign them off early, or refuse to sign. This is very often threatened, all day long, but almost never done. Poor things, they are the absolute bottom of the acting profession, but some of them have a pathetic desire to be appreciated. Quite a few get steady work, especially if they are chosen to be a stand-in. Most of them have other professions to keep them

going. The oldest are in their 70s – wise, benevolent, seen it all, and looked up to by the young ones. They are successful career extras! But a lot of the ladies look like ageing nightclub hostesses, and the men like street buskers. Quite depressing.

Today we had to get them all done up like a 1911 Coronation crowd. Then they had to be individually vetted to make sure they weren't wearing modern spectacles, watches and so on. Finally they were arranged in a long stand lining the roadside. The 'roadside' was actually a track for the camera to run on with a wide column at either end. The camera rode down this on a 'dolly', panning past the waving, cheering crowd, from column to column. Then we 'cut', re-arranged the crowd, pulled the camera back to its original position, and did it again. By splicing the film, or mixing from shot to shot, as the camera went past a column, the crowd could appear to be as large and long as was needed. It will be projected behind the coach with SLO and MM in it on its way to the Abbey.

Needless to say, when we filled the stand, it was only half full. David roared and stamped and we all went off like hounds, in search of the rest. The men's lavatories yielded 14, playing cards, with a bottle of whisky between them. Many threats and pleadings later they were on parade. The ladies' lavatories were the same. There was even a card game going on under the stand itself. The canteen, which was off limits as they will be given lunch boxes, had almost 30! At last we got about enough and we stopped counting. (They are very adept at confusing a count to protect their 'mates'.)

David and I and another two second assistant directors yelled and applauded and waved and cheered to encourage them to do the same. Then we mixed them up and did it again. It was a lovely sunny day, which helped us a lot, but apparently that is a very *bad* thing for the film. It seems we have some real Coronation footage (Elizabeth II) which will be cut in with our footage to make it more impressive, and of course on QE's

Coronation it never stopped raining, so the two footages might not match. How perverse.

We did the whole operation about 10 times, until everyone was fed up, not to say rebellious. We then took the opportunity to audition some of them for the ballroom scene, in a rehearsal room with a piano. We will need a mass of dancers for the Grand Ball, and we can get them from ballroom dancing clubs, but NOT until every member of the FAA who can put one foot in front of another to music has been given a chance. Otherwise we will have a strike. They all want to work, so many of them claimed to be experts, but in the end we took only eight couples, and they are not much cop. It was a sop to the union to take any at all, but hopefully they won't be noticed in a crowd of professionals.

SUNDAY, 2 SEPTEMBER

Last night, after an excellent dinner, Tony told me of a rumour that MM was pregnant!! He is very alarmed. Will we soon have to cope with morning sickness, depression etc. as well as everything else? He wanted me to try to check it out with the household before he told SLO and started a panic. So this morning I rang Plod and went over to Parkside for a quiet chat, on the pretext of talking to the staff. (They are restless, as usual.) Plod was very jolly. He would confirm nothing but just put a finger beside his nose with his lips sealed. I'm not quite sure if this means 'yes' or 'no', but I assume 'yes'. Plod is the only one who never seems to be affected by the lunacy going on all round him. As he is now more loyal to MM than to me, and quite rightly so, I couldn't ask for details. Plod and I are close, but MM is his employer. She never speaks to him. He's like a stout walking-stick for her to lean on and he's very happy just to be that.

Paula appeared, looking as if she was trying to keep calm in a whirlwind. I sympathise with her. She has definitely bitten off more than she can chew. In the beginning, it was Milton who undertook to deliver MM's person, and Paula who undertook to deliver her performance. Now they are both facing failure. The whole film – and a lot of money – depends on their success but they both seem to have run out of ideas.

AM has left the country, and Hedda Rosten is no help at all. Plod says she encourages MM to drink champagne with her at all hours of the day. Naturally this makes MM feel ghastly and so she starts hitting the pills. There is no discipline whatsoever, and when Paula and Milton try to impose some, they become very unpopular and have to back off to survive. Hopeless.

I came back and told Tony there was no truth in the rumour about the pregnancy. Why give SLO another worry when there is nothing we can do about it? If the rumour does turn out to be true, we will all simply have to adapt as best we can, or the film will grind to a halt.

MONDAY, 3 SEPTEMBER

Once again, MM surprised us. Today she was inspired to make an enormous effort by the music. She has two music scenes in the film and they are being shot 'back to back'. The first was her dance to the music of a barrel organ, which was coming in through the open windows of the purple room. Richard Addinsell has written two pretty tunes for her, and this one is light and happy. MM is, as always, in that gorgeous white figure-hugging creation of Bumble's, and it is perfect for dancing.

The dances in this film are all 'choreographed' by Billy Chappell.* He is as camp as coffee but he is very sweet and cosy and gets on well with MM. All in all it was a delightful scene and MM did it exquisitely. The dance is interrupted by the

* Chappell (b.1908) started out as a dancer with the Rambert company. He went on to design ballets, light reviews and plays.

young King, Jeremy Spenser, and it was easy to see that he was genuinely impressed by MM's performance. He is now almost the only person whom MM still likes, so it ended up a successful day.

One has to remember that even though MM is making a film with SLO, it is up to MM to make it something special – a super-star creation. SLO has made many films – some great and some mouldy. Only on stage, to a very limited audience, can he be seen as the great actor he is. And MM is carrying quite a lot of other burdens as well – a husband who is unsupportive, and away; a manager who could be seen as exploiting her; and 'best friends' who are sycophantic and weak. 'Ruth amid the alien corn' really. MM rose to where she is now by being stronger, more talented and more ambitious than the competition. I dread to think how many blonde bombshells there are in Hollywood right now, trying to get where MM got by any means, fair or foul.

Whenever I meet anyone who has got right to the top, I always notice that they have something extra that ordinary people – including me alas – do not have. And that 'little extra', whatever it is, does not mean that they have a happy or an easy life – quite the contrary. We have no right to demand that they share that little extra with us and then criticise them for being different or difficult or 'dangerous to know'. MM has more than a little extra, and yet the technicians expect her to behave like a twopenny Rank starlet. If I was SLO I would tell them off, and lay out the red carpet for MM every day. But that would mean telling himself off too, and admitting that while he is great in many ways, it is MM who is the MOVIE STAR.

TUESDAY, 4 SEPTEMBER

Inspired by the success of the dance scene, MM was in a more confident mood than I have seen her for some time. The set was declared 'closed' (i.e. no spectators) – as if it had ever been open. This was because MM had to sing the whole of the Sleeping Prince Waltz to SLO, in a close two-shot.

It did at least mean a minimum of hangers-on, with no Drapes, Chippies, Plasterers and Props, who are usually hanging around, 'just in case'. Those who were essential but not absolutely essential – i.e. most people – were kept firmly out of sight. MM was kneeling over SLO on the purple sofa, in the purple room. She had quite a long, difficult speech, leading into the song. SLO was prepared to break it down into two extra shots. Instead of one shot for the whole scene it could have been made up of a close-up of SLO, a close-up of MM, and then the two-shot favouring MM for the song, but this wasn't necessary. Earlier, when the Grand Duke wanted to seduce Elsie Marina, he had arranged for his valet to play the violin in the corridor. Now it was Elsie's turn to seduce the Grand Duke, and she arranged for a veritable orchestra of valets and footmen in the corridor, all waiting to play on her cue.

Close-up Grand Duke (genuinely puzzled): 'Where's that music coming from?' (He knew he hadn't laid it on this time.)

Two-shot favouring MM. MM giggles: 'Oh never mind. It's just that Hungarian, I expect.' (She knows now that the 'Hungarian' had really been the valet.) 'You told me he plays every night.' She paused and sang the waltz:

> 'I found a dream, I laid in your arms,
> The whole night through,
> I'm yours, no matter what others may say or do...

'My sweet . . .' she said and gave SLO a passionate kiss.

It was very good – singing *and* acting, and indeed the scene went on for another couple of speeches. For the first time MM behaved like a trouper. She is really happiest when she sings. Perhaps it is because it is a nice uncomplicated thing to do, something she often does when she is alone, or frightened.

In the previous films she's always seemed a rather reluctant chanteuse, but not this time. I should add that she didn't have to sing the final version. Today's voice will not be in the film – that will be 'post-synched' in the sound studio much later. But her lip movements today will be vital so she had to sing properly, nonetheless. And she did, in fact, give a performance which impressed everyone. What a pity SLO can't build on this, but it is really too late. After lunch, things weren't quite so easy. MM had to declare her passion – 'Oh gosh, your Grand Ducal Highness, how I love you' – and throw herself into his arms. Then they were interrupted by the hapless Dicky W, once again with a phoney excuse, this time on the Duke's behalf.

I don't know if MM had had a drink in the break, or a pill, or both. (MM loves champers but she does not ever drink too much on its own.) Anyway she seemed to be on another plane. She was jolly enough, but communication got more and more difficult. By the end of the day, when she had only one close-up left to do, she had become wistfully sad – and completely lost. Her only line was 'I didn't quite catch that' – referring to the Duke's declaration of love in Carpathian – but even that was almost impossible for her to say. The hair got tousled, the red rashes came and went. Then, suddenly, she got it right, like catching a butterfly in mid-flight. I do see why directors dread working with her, poor lady. You never know *which* MM you will get next – or how long it might take to get anything at all.

WEDNESDAY, 5 SEPTEMBER

They have finished building the Grand Duke's dressing room, which leads into the purple room. This means there are a lot more scenes we can now shoot without MM. She did not turn up until lunch, and again she wasn't in very good shape. If she hasn't arrived by 9 a.m., and I haven't been able to learn from Plod when she is due to leave Parkside, I have to go to help David in the studio. I don't know until lunchtime whether she is there or not. It is academic really because she needs to be in Make-up before 9.30 for any work to be done with her before the lunchbreak.

This morning we did the follow-up to the Grand Duke's attempted seduction. Elsie has passed out and four footmen have been summoned to carry her into a bedroom. The sleepy valet, who has been dragged out of bed to play his violin, wanders into the drawing room, still fiddling away, gawping with curiosity. The part is played by a little old Greek actor called Andrea Melandrinos. It was hard to tell whether he was acting or really in a dream. When SLO yelled at him to shut up, he jumped out of his skin exactly like a real servant would have done and the crew dissolved into laughter. Neither he nor SLO could decide whether to be pleased or not by this comic success. The shot had to be done several times, and was never quite so funny again.

In the afternoon we did MM's long silent walk around SLO. He is being shaved by the same valet and is totally preoccupied. Elsie comes out of the bedroom in the background, walks through the purple room, into the dressing room, takes a cup of coffee, walks right round the Grand Duke and returns to the bedroom. She was draped in a pink bedspread, totally dishevelled with her blonde hair (a different wig) hanging loose down her back. The Grand Duke only does a double-take as the

bedroom door shuts. For some reason, this scene bothered MM
a lot. Perhaps it was a situation with which she could identify
all too closely? She had no lines to remember but, in her confused state, even little details like when to collect the cup of
coffee gave her maximum trouble. And, wrapped up as she was,
it wasn't easy to carry anything. Although the camera could
hardly see her face, her general appearance was frightful. Her
walk, however, was unmistakable, especially from behind. If
that wiggle of the rear end comes out on camera, the film will
be saved!

Finally we did the shot of her collapsed on the bed, under
the pink coverlet, where Dicky discovers her and, presumably,
wakes her, before that walk. There was nothing anyone could
do to make this shot presentable. The truth was that she just
looked like a tart, the morning after. It is a very hard thing to
define, but I've seen it (to my shame), and SLO could certainly
recognise it too. No amount of fussing by drapes and set
dressers could alter it. Something in the way MM sprawled on
the bed, I guess. We'll see in rushes tomorrow.

I just can't see how MM can keep this up all week. She looks
shattered, washed out, in a dream. LOP and MMP have a huge
insurance policy in case SLO or MM are ill. Filming must be
stopped for five days before they pay and an independent doctor
has to examine the 'ill' person. Mental illness does not count.
Of course this does not apply to MM yet, but SLO had Mr P
check the policy because he can see the writing on the wall.
The most difficult question is – what will make MM recover
her composure? What will help her to start working properly
again? AM is not due back for a week. Plod says MM phones
him in NYC for hours and hours, but that does not seem to
make her any better – sometimes worse! And what if she is
pregnant? Suddenly it looks possible that the film will never be
finished . . . and we are only four weeks in.

THURSDAY, 6 SEPTEMBER

Sure enough, at 10 a.m. we had an official message from Parkside to say MM was not well, and a doctor had been called. I reported this to SLO. He wanted to know which doctor. A local GP? A specialist in nervous diseases? There was quite a difference. I rang Plod and spoke to Hedda. AM had found the name of a London physician from a friend and had recommended him over the phone. Hedda had arranged for him to call that afternoon. But whatever he says, Hedda thinks that MM will not return to the studio before next Wednesday (Sept 12th). As AM returns from NYC next Tuesday (Sept 11th) this seems a likely guess.

Milton arrived late. He had been to Parkside, and even he had been kept waiting for an hour. He and SLO immediately went into conference, frantically calculating whether a claim could be made on the insurance, and how to get the insurance company to examine MM for a second opinion (some hope!). I do not know if it would be necessary to shut the film down for five days in order for a claim to succeed. Presumably we would all still be paid – by the insurance company. But such an interruption is a horrendous thought. In the meantime, there are cut-away shots to be done with SLO, and scenes in the dressing room with SLO, Dicky, and Jeremy Spenser. Most of these are done very quickly and efficiently, with the only delays being for moving the camera and relighting. But they filled today and will fill tomorrow too. Mr P and Teddy Joseph have arranged for a day on location at the Foreign Office (the real one) for Monday which means a lot of work for the Ast Dirs. The road outside the FO in St James's Park has to be closed from very early in the morning, and filled with horses and carriages and extras dressed as passers-by. Everyone concerned is being very helpful. Even though MM is not going to be there herself, her name alone always works magic.

The dressing-room set is much more sympathetic than the purple room, although it may not be so dramatic on camera. It is a bedroom/dressing room which must have been quite rare in 1911 in such a large mansion as the Carpathian Embassy in Belgrave Square. Since this script is taken from a play in which all the action took place in one room, and it has been stretched to take place in one house, the rooms must interconnect. SLO has many changes of extremely handsome military-style uniforms – but somehow they do not suit him. He has chosen an ultra-teutonic bearing for the Grand Duke, his short hair slicked down, his collar buttoned up to his chin and a monocle in his eye. This worked well with Vivien on stage. She knew exactly how to play against it, and she could melt your heart with her combination of bright intelligence and vulnerability. (She certainly melted mine.) But with MM – as naive and well-intentioned as a puppy – the Grand Duke seems stiff to the point of absurdity. He never seems to relax. I don't know if that is in the script or because SLO feels so unhappy. It certainly takes away the romantic appeal and makes Elsie falling in love with the Duke stretch credulity to the limits. We can already see this in the 'rushes'. Of course Tony B is full of 'how wonderful Laurence is' but I feel there isn't enough for SLO to get his teeth into. Rather, the role has got its teeth into him. He gives the impression of a director who has walked onto the set and into the leading role. And that isn't make-believe – which is what the film is meant to be about – it is exactly what has happened.

FRIDAY, 7 SEPTEMBER

Another long scene of the Grand Duke being shaved, in his bedroom/dressing room, by Andrea Melandrinos, the valet who played the violin. Since he still behaves exactly like a valet, one must now assume he is a brilliant actor. There is another valet, played by Dennis Edwards, who is tall and thin, and quiet to the point of seeming in another world. When Elsie Marina, wrapped only in a bedspread, did her long walk round the Duke, Dennis was directed to stare in amazement. The trouble is that in the meantime, no one has told Dennis to stop staring in amazement. So all through today's scene, when nothing untoward is happening so far as he is concerned, there he is, still staring in amazement. SLO couldn't see him, of course, because he is acting in the scene, and Tony B did not notice. I must admit that I was not brave enough to point out the problem, so it will be in the movie. It is not the job of the assistant directors to assist the director to direct. Years ago I was invited, by Vivien I suppose, onto the set of *Caesar and Cleopatra*.* Gaby Pascal was directing a crowd scene. Caesar's troops had just landed in Alexandria or something, and the people were in a panic. After a couple of takes, I pointed out to Pascal that quite a few of them were just wandering around, looking blank. I now know that this was because he hadn't told them what to do. Extras who are not told what to do wander around and look blank. But my observations were not well received – (I was 12 at the time) – so I didn't risk repeating my mistake. When I am a director . . .

SATURDAY, 8 SEPTEMBER

Plod called me over to Parkside for a chat. He could say nothing directly, but he hinted that MM had been pregnant but had now miscarried. The baby must have been no more than a month. This seems very young to be called 'a baby' but I know nothing about pregnancy, I must admit. Plod is very concerned. He adores MM now, even though she doesn't seem to notice that

* Vivien Leigh played Cleopatra in the 1945 screen adaptation of Shaw's play, at the time the most expensive British film ever made.

he exists. (You never know with MM, she has very good peripheral vision.)

'Does anyone else know?' I asked.

'Milton Greene, I suppose.'

'Does Arthur?'

'I don't think so, no.'

So much for marriage!

I went over to Tibbs Farm to check it out. When I arrived, Milton and Amy were in a dreadful state. Josh, their son, had fallen out of their car as they were going down the driveway. A doctor was with him, but, amazingly, he wasn't hurt, just very shocked. Poor little guy. For once Milton wasn't remotely concerned with MM. They assumed that I had heard the news about Josh, and come over to sympathise about that. So I said nothing about Plod's news and I never will. I just hope MM recovers. She must have had a pretty bad shock too, if Plod is right.

MONDAY, 17 SEPTEMBER

I haven't written for a whole week and I feel bad about it. We've had a very difficult five days in the studio. It is dark outside when I arrive at 6.45 a.m. – dark, cold and depressing. The addition of the Grand Duke's dressing room to the purple room did not give us the boost I hoped for.

Jack Harris, the editor, has started to visit every day which makes SLO nervous. There is nothing so bad as finding you have a gap in the film which can't be covered by another shot. If actors hesitate, or click with their teeth or let their eyes flick off-camera it can look very embarrassing when blown up on the screen. When you watch rushes you see so many mistakes and overlaps that it is easy to miss the ones that you can't cover. Only the editor can tell this, as he starts to build up the 'rough cut'. Retakes are very expensive, because you can't afford to keep all the big sets built, 'just in case'. So Jack has to be absolutely sure that all is well before the purple set is destroyed. We will certainly store a small corner of it and then we will have something in reserve.

Poor MM has been very depressed. She missed Monday and Tuesday altogether as forecast. She seemed pretty drugged on Wednesday despite AM's return. We soldier on, getting a good take here, and an adequate take there. The rushes have become much less reassuring. We can only see the agony it took to get the shot, and the confusion in MM's eyes. Even so, MM looks just as beautiful. When she is on the screen you can't take your eyes off her. Tomorrow we will start in the big new hall and staircase set in Studio B. Let us hope we all get a new lease of life. If it wasn't for Anne and Tony, I don't think I would have survived.

TUESDAY, 18 SEPTEMBER

The Embassy hall and staircase set is almost as hideous as the purple drawing room, but not as claustrophobic. Neither set *should* be claustrophobic at all. They are opened up to allow the camera in, dissected one way or another, and set down in this vast, aircraft hangar of a studio. However when three sides of a set are built and the camera, sound, lighting and production crews all squeeze into the fourth side, it feels very cramped. The ceiling is 40 feet up but it is impossible to see past the bright lights hanging down, and they get very hot, so the effect is like working in an underground power station.

The design of the hall is quite impressive. It is a bit like a set for a 19th-century operetta, and I suppose that is intentional. In the script, when Dicky enters with Elsie Marina for the first time, he says 'Personally I find the decorations a little vulgar,' which must have given Roger Furse a good clue.

The walls in the bottom half are pale blue, and above the

Vivien Leigh overcome by Carpathian vodka and champagne in
The Sleeping Prince. Paul Hardwick (right) played the Major Domo in
both the play and the film.

MM about to be overcome in *The Prince and the Showgirl*. Paul
Hardwick's costume has acquired rather more gold braid for the film.

MM and SLO surrounded by dancing club extras in the ballroom scene.
MM genuinely loved to dance.

The young King (Jeremy Spenser) watches Elsie Marina doing her very charming dance routine in the purple sitting room.

The coach about to jolt into motion. All but Dame Sybil are already tensed in anticipation.

Production unit photograph of
The Prince and the Showgirl.

1 Wardrobe Mistress
2 SLO's stand-in
3 MM's dresser
4 MM's stand-in
5 David Orton, 1st Assistant
  Director
6 Unit Photographer
7 Jack Cardiff, Lighting
  Cameraman
8 MM
9 SLO
10 Denys Coop, Camera Operator
11 Tony Bushell, Associate Director
12 John Mitchell, Sound Man
13 Elaine Schreyck, Continuity
14 Carmen Dillon, Art Director
15 Lighting Gaffer
16 Beatrice Dawson, Costume
   Designer

17 Jack Harris, Film Editor
18 Production Secretary
19 Teddy Joseph, Production Manager
20 Gordon Bond, Hair Stylist
21 SLO's dresser
22 Colin Clark
23 Roger Furse's assistant
24 Vanessa Matthew, Mr Perceval's secretary
25 Geoff Haines, 2nd Assistant Director

MM, standing between
Victor Mature and
Anthony Quayle,
meets the Queen at the
Royal film premiere of
*The Battle of the River
Plate.* MM and HM
were almost exactly
the same age.

stairs they are lilac. In these walls are round alcoves, painted black, with white plaster busts, like some travesty of Wedgwood. All the columns are marbled to death, and so are the steps and the door surrounds. But the wide double staircase has a good sweep to it, and the gallery running round the top has a pleasing dimension. The whole thing could have been designed for dramatic entrances and exits (*à la* Evelyn Laye*), although there aren't any of these in our film. Four footmen are usually stationed in this hall, in costumes as exaggerated as the decor. It is they who will be summoned to carry Miss Marina to the spare bedroom when she passes out. The Embassy exterior, which we will shoot on the 'lot', is a copy of the Portuguese Embassy in Belgrave Square. (I wonder what that building looked like inside in 1911 – or looks like now for that matter. I must ask Roger if he's seen it.)

When I am not running David's errands, or standing beside SLO in case he wants a cigarette – (I am official cigarette bearer) – I spend most of the time gossiping with Paul H (the Major Domo) and Dicky W. Dicky has his own chair – what luxury – as his is really the third most important part in the film. Paul is very good at commandeering one too as his costume is tight. He is in a great many scenes and his face is wonderfully expressive even though he hardly ever speaks. They have a few hilarious scenes between them. When Dicky arrives the morning after Elsie has passed out, Paul rushes to tell him the news – that the chorus girl is still in the Embassy. Then Paul adds a *sotto voce* – and obviously vulgar – joke and Dicky freezes him with his sternest look. It was done so economically and understatedly that it was a delight to watch. Exactly what Rattigan had in mind, I am sure.

Dicky and Paul can swap jokes all day – theatrical jokes, camp jokes, drinking jokes. They are very enjoyable company

* b.1900. British musical comedy star, chiefly on stage.

and they prefer me as an audience to the crew. (I am much more likely to know the people involved.) Tony B joins in sometimes, but when the jokes get risqué – which is very often – he gives them the same look Dicky gave Paul in the film, and marches off. Dicky and Paul also drink a great deal together in the evenings. I was in the men's lavatories this morning, and all the time I was standing there, the most appalling noise, of retching and defecating, came out of one of the stalls. Then, as I was washing my hands, out came Paul.

'Morning, my boy' he said cheerily, as he marched off into the studio. I was expecting someone to call for an ambulance. What a constitution these actors have.

WEDNESDAY, 19 SEPTEMBER

AM returned yesterday, and by midday today he had been universally cast as villain of the piece. SLO is cross because he had hoped that AM would help MM to turn over a new leaf, and this clearly has not happened. She arrived at the studio late and demanding. In fact she is clearly fed up with AM and also disenchanted with Milton whom she cuts dead. She complained about her dress, and her hair, and her make-up, which is very unusual for her.

It is also pointless, since Elaine, the continuity girl, has absolute control over how she looks now. Elaine has to keep track of exactly how everyone looked in the preceding shot even though it may have been filmed at a totally different time. If MM even ruffles her hair a tiny bit, there could be a mismatch in the final film, and Elaine is determined that such a thing will never happen.* Like all the crew, she has to be a perfectionist or she might as well not bother to turn up at all. Film discipline is that strict.

* It never did.

Milton blames AM for the change in MM's attitude, both to her work and to him. Milton is in a very difficult position. He wants to control MM and her career, but he has to get this film finished on time and on budget if MMP, and he, is to make money (not to mention LOP and Warner Bros). And this means he has to co-operate with SLO and all of us, even at the risk of upsetting MM. So it is easy for someone (AM) to poison MM's mind against him.

Paula is treated by AM with extreme disdain. I have heard him describe Paula as a charlatan to Milton in SLO's dressing room and I'm sure he does it in front of MM. This is hard luck on MM since she totally depends on Paula when AM is away. She has no one else except the tipsy Hedda. Finally AM is not above snide remarks about Milton to Paula, which quickly get repeated, so Milton gets upset even though he has nothing concrete to go on. What a crew.

This evening MM told Milton that she was not satisfied with her car. She wants it replaced with a new Jaguar (a Mk VII saloon I suppose). This seemed pretty reasonable to me. A star like MM ought to be able to travel in any car she wants. Think of Gary Cooper's Duesenberg. SLO just shrugged, but to Milton, and to Tony B, it is an affront. They can see the dark hand of AM at work. Who will pay for it, MMP or LOP? As part of the British production obligations, it should be LOP. But it is for MM's special use, so it should be MMP. 'He is trying to pull a fast one. He wants us to buy it and then he will ship it over (Right-hand drive??) to the USA for his own private use.'* And they were livid. I think it is funnier that a left-wing intellectual should want to drive round in a Jaguar with Marilyn Monroe. (Although didn't Lenin have a Rolls-Royce?) That is not the point, said Milton and Tony B, together, when I teased them. 'AM is going to ruin the movie.'

---

* They did get the Jaguar, but it was unreliable and I don't know if they took it back to the USA or not.

Actually the problem with the Jaguar will be that it has no glass division between the passenger compartment and the driver. I think Plod likes the peacefulness of the front of the Princess.

MM left the studios in a huff. She does not like being crossed when she has made her wishes clear; no more than any other film star before her. Quite right too, I say, but Plod looked gloomy.

THURSDAY, 20 SEPTEMBER

Today SLO took MM as far as he possibly could and then even further. He was directing only, not being in the scenes himself, so he was more in control than usual. We were in the hall and staircase set and he had planned a long-shot on the stairs, a continuation of MM's arrival at the Embassy with Dicky, her Foreign Office escort.

In the end it took 29 takes before we got it right. 29 takes is an historic amount, even for MM. I really think SLO wanted to break all records as proof, actual visible proof, of how difficult it is to work with her. It was a complicated shot, with the camera on a big crane following MM and Dicky up the stairs and walking round the gallery into the door of the purple room. (The actual purple room was in Studio A, of course, and is now destroyed.)

David: 'Going for a take. QUIET studio please.'

'Lights.' Clunk.

'Camera running.'

'Sound.' Beep beep.

'Speed.'

'Mark it.'

'*Prince and the Showgirl*. Shot 137 take 1.' Clap.

'Action.'

Dicky W: 'This way, Miss Marina.' (His voice combines

disapproval with resignation.) They climb the stairs. MM looks around, asks about dinner, asks about the Grand Duke's wife ('Passed over' says Dicky). They reach the gallery. Dicky starts to explain which Royal Personage she might meet and how to address each one.

MM: 'Wow, I'm shaking. This is worse than a first night.' Exeunt. CUT.

Repeat 29 times!

Everyone was frantic. MM's rash came and went. Each time the camera was difficult to reposition correctly and the cameraman, Denys, was grey with fatigue. It is a big set and needs a lot of lights, so the lighting crew up on the gantry was nearly cooked. We could have broken the shot down into two or three shorter bits by shooting close-ups of reactions on MM and Dicky, to be cut in later. But SLO had the bit between his teeth, so on and on we went. Dicky is incredibly professional and he never wavers, or misses a word. But he was sweating so much in that hot braided uniform that he must have lost several pounds of weight.

MM simply could not remember all her lines, and when she did remember, she did not say them correctly. The lines were often silly and inconsequential and there were many changes of thought and direction. It is true that they were the sort of things one might say, going up the stairs to supper in a strange house, with strange people, but it was quite a risky challenge to put them all in one long continuous take.

As they went up the stairs, MM had to say 'Think of the trouble of bringing the food all the way up from the kitchen.'

Dicky replied: 'I fancy it will be a cold supper, Miss Marina.'

MM: 'They still have to bring it, don't they?' Then a change of thought: 'Is his wife still alive?' etc.

This sort of dialogue is written to illustrate Elsie's charming naiveté and it could have worked. When MM blurted it out, having just (only just) remembered it in time, it did not sound 'off the cuff', even to her. So then she started to forget the other lines, one by one, almost as if she wanted to wipe them out. Back she would go to Paula, hands flapping as if she was hoping to fly. There was much whispering, much looking at the script as if they were trying to translate it from a foreign language, and then back to the set for another try.

Amazingly enough we did get the shot on take 29, but at what cost we will not know until later. In his dressing room, SLO admitted to Milton that he should have broken the scene down. But by this time MM and Paula were speeding home in what mental state one could only guess at. For the record, and perhaps this influenced SLO, we had filmed virtually the same shot in the morning only with Dicky and Paul going up the stairs and meeting Jeremy Spenser in the gallery. We had done that in four takes, the first three having had minor camera problems.

FRIDAY, 21 SEPTEMBER

Today the hall and stairs set was readjusted so that we could shoot MM and Dicky going *down* the stairs.

It went much better, mainly because MM only had one thought in the scene – namely to escape the clutches of the Grand Duke. The exercise of authority by SLO yesterday seemed to have a good effect, to Milton's surprise. After all, we did get the shot. MM respects authority as much as she fights against it. Her relationship with SLO seemed a little more professional at last, and as a result the filming was easier and quicker. Of course there were problems. In her hasty exit from the purple drawing room, Elsie Marina had tried frantically to get her coat on, and failed. We shot this scene a couple of weeks ago and Elaine had noted it and had the film to prove it. MM's 'coat' is a frilly, lilac, silk taffeta affair which looks most elegant and becoming when it is on. But it is almost impossible to slip into in a hurry. So when MM emerges into the corridor at high speed, she still has to have it twisted round one arm. There was no real problem with this but it is the sort of thing that can easily put MM off. In the event it all went smoothly, and MM did manage to get the coat on over the next few shots, without letting it interrupt her thought processes. Dicky is an absolute rock, but alas MM treats him like a non-person. (This is how she treats most of us now.) She is in so many scenes with Dicky that it would have been a great help if she could have got cosy with him. Perhaps it is because he is queer, and doesn't look at her the way most men do. I don't mean that he is in the least effeminate, but I'm sure she can tell, and that makes him a 'non-man'. Of course he is also quintessentially British, and that is not her favourite nationality right now.

After lunch we filmed Dicky trying to persuade Elsie Marina to stay for her supper engagement. MM is convinced the Regent is only out to seduce her: 'He's a Carpathian Grand Duke, for heaven's sake.'

Dicky: 'Educated in England.'

MM: 'That's just what I mean.'

All this went on as they dodged around the marble columns in the hall, Dicky desperately pulling MM back onto her camera marks as she blundered about. But it worked again, and when we saw the four printed takes from yesterday's historic labours, MM looked lovely, acted well, and stole the scene. Let that be added to the story of 'the 29 takes'.

SUNDAY, 23 SEPTEMBER

Phew, what a weekend. I certainly celebrated my 24th birthday (in two weeks, actually) with a bang. On Friday night I had made a date to go out on a 'pub-crawl' with Dicky and Paul. We spend hours and hours gossiping on the set every day, and we all enjoy each other's company, but the outside world changes things. After a few drinks it became obvious that all Dicky wanted to do was pick up some gorgeous hunk of a man, and all Paul wanted to do was to get drunk out of his mind. I don't disapprove of either of these activities but I wanted dinner too, so we went to a 'bistro' Dicky knew in Soho. It was a queer's bar really. The food was delicious and I ate it, but Dicky just flirted and Paul just drank. (I don't know if Paul is queer or not. There's no Mrs Paul as far as I know, so maybe.) Just as we were wondering where to go next, in came Gordon Alexander, the dresser, camp as coffee as usual. He knew a very special and very exciting place, he said – giving me the eye, I noticed – so we all piled into a taxi and set off. Going along Piccadilly, Dicky got completely hysterical. He lay on the floor and said he was going to die. He and Paul were completely drunk by now, so we stopped the cab and tumbled them both out onto the pavement.

'Drive on!' screamed Gordon at the cabbie, who was only too relieved to do so. 'Thank goodness we've got rid of those two old queens,' said Gordon, putting his hand on my knee. 'Let's go home and you can fuck me.'

Peter P-M* used to talk like this so I'm used to it, although I wish he had closed the taxi-driver window first!

'I'm not sure I want to do that,' I said. (I was sure I didn't.)

'We'll go back and have a nightcap anyway,' said Gordon, giving the driver new instructions. Gordon's flat was really very nicely done up – watercolours, comfy sofas, pretty lamps etc. Gordon brought some gin ('Gordon's' he said, giggling) but he had no cigarettes and I had run out hours ago which made me nervous.

'Never mind,' said Gordon, grabbing me by the crotch. 'I'll

* Peter Pitt Milward owned a castle called Paco da Gloria in northern Portugal. I had spent the previous summer there. In 1978 Peter died, and I acquired the castle and lived there, off and on, until 1987.

give you a nice blow job.' I had heard this phrase before, but I didn't know exactly what it meant. It sounded sexy, so I said OK. It felt great to start with but in the end I got restless and found it unsatisfactory. Gordon seemed to be having more fun than I was. I don't really like sex unless I can take an active part. However it all worked out in the end, and Gordon seemed grateful.

'We must do that again,' he said. I'm not so sure.

I slept really late yesterday and then went to the Stork Club again. Yvonne was there with somebody else, but I persuaded her to join me after they left, and took her straight home. I just had to have normal sex again. I've grown out of all that school-boy stuff at last. Perhaps I'll go back to it when I'm old, but for now I prefer girls. I saw Al* this evening but I didn't tell him what was going on. The film world is different, I suppose. It's more exciting, and I've got a hangover to prove it!

MONDAY, 24 SEPTEMBER

Back at work in the hall set, taking it apart and putting it back again so we can film it from every angle. I have been having a feud with MM's stand-in. She and SLO's stand-in are always in the studio, on call every day, and they are meant to arrive at the same time as the stars. After a quick visit to make-up and wardrobe, they must be on the set by 8 a.m., ready for lighting to begin. It is a thankless task. They just stand where they are told and move where they are told, while they are lit as if they were the stars and their moves are 'plotted' by camera and sound. They never get the chance to perform, even if the star is ill, like an understudy does in the theatre. They are generally considered to be at the very bottom of the studio pecking order, only just above the 'extras' who make up the

* Alan, my older brother.

crowd scenes, and from whose ranks they have been drawn. I
suppose I look at them the way Terry Rattigan looks at me –
(which is also the way MM looks at Terry Rattigan!). MM's
stand-in is a pretty little thing, but half MM's size and with
none of her personality. Now she has taken to arriving late in
the mornings too. Not as late as MM, of course, or she would
be fired instantly, but 25 minutes late is a lot for a stand-in.

I am responsible to David for getting the right people on the
right set at the right time. With MM this is difficult, but with
the stand-ins it should be automatic. Indeed, they are usually
so anxious to please, and be hired again, that they are early.
The MM girl has not taken any notice of my stern rebukes.
This morning she even threatened to get me into trouble for
being rude – which I expect I was. I will have to investigate
this a little further. When a girl like that starts getting cheeky,
it usually means she has some powerful man to protect her –
I have deep suspicions.

TUESDAY, 25 SEPTEMBER

I got the 2nd Ast Dir to cover me at the Star Dressing Room
entrance after SLO had arrived, taking a fairly certain gamble
on MM being at least an hour late. Then I went round to the
main entrance and waited out of sight. Sure enough, at 7.30,
Jack Cardiff drove up, and the MM stand-in hopped out of his
car. She waved goodbye before she hurried inside, and Jack
went off to park. There is no law against giving stand-ins a lift
to the studio, but now I knew why she could afford to be
cheeky. Jack, as lighting cameraman, is the most important man
in the studio after SLO. It is he who is responsible for how the
film looks, after SLO has decided what it should contain. Jack
is also especially important to MM. It is he who makes her look
so beautiful. She also likes him and respects him. He is indeed
a very charming and likeable man, although I don't know him

that well. It is not up to me to criticise him if he makes a friend. But it is my job to get stand-ins on the set on time, even if it is really Jack who will be kept waiting if they are not. David feels very strongly that just because MM is always late, the rest of the studio must not be allowed to get slack. I decided not to tell David what I had seen, but when the MM girl came on the set, late again, I gave her a pretty firm rebuke. I did it in front of Jack in the hope that he might realise that he must get her to work earlier. That was not a success. Jack was livid. He told me that, as lighting cameraman, stand-ins were his prob-lem, and to mind my own business. David just blinked like an owl, and motioned me out of the studio. He didn't want to have a row in front of the crew, and told me that he would have a quiet word with Jack later. For the rest of the day, there was a considerable coolness between Jack and myself. I am sure he won't mention it to SLO, but I am only the 3rd Ast Dir; and 3rd Ast Dirs are not expected to upset lighting cameramen. Luckily Tony didn't notice anything. He never does, bless him, unless SLO is involved.

WEDNESDAY, 26 SEPTEMBER

Dame Sybil came into the studio again today. I was wearing her red scarf as usual, and she gave me a huge hello. It was nice to see her again and MM was thrilled – a visit from Grandma! Having been warned, MM was even almost on time. Dame S is now acting in a West End play, which means she doesn't finish until 11 p.m. at night, but there she was in her hire car at 7 a.m., beaming and smiling. We filmed her making the Grand Duke give Elsie Marina a Carpathian medal, the one which he had just given the Ambassador. ('Such quibbles,' when he objects!) We could not do it earlier because the hall hadn't been built. Her character in the film is as sympathetic as she is, deaf to anything she doesn't want to hear. When Elsie says

'Oui' she is quite convinced that she can speak fluent French.

MM was in top form, bouncy and jolly. Her appearance, off camera, changes with her mood. When she is happy she looks really attractive. One can see what all the fuss is about. She is only 29* and she certainly has a wonderful figure. She doesn't even need a bra in that amazing white dress. With Dame S she behaves like a schoolgirl, and an obedient schoolgirl at that. Jack has started to play up to MM much more too, which helps. Alas, it is too late for SLO to react. If he could only strengthen her confidence somehow, reinforce it when it is high. But Plod tells me that Lee Strasberg calls her every evening from the USA – reverse charge of course – and this undermines SLO a lot. I mentioned this to Milton. He also hates the Strasbergs but by now he seems powerless to prevent their influence. At least Milton's son, Josh, is OK after the accident. But MM seems to be slipping from his grasp.

THURSDAY, 27 SEPTEMBER

We continue with reaction shots of MM in the hall – her first impression of the Embassy, her meeting with the Grand Duke, and the scene where Dicky reassures her that he will save her from a fate worse than death. She seemed less clear in the head today and more woozy. I hope Milton isn't giving her too many pills again. It's one of the ways he can still control her. Milton now has an assistant called David Maysles.** David looks like a young American college undergraduate. He has a great deal of ambition and this makes him irreverent and mischievous. He frequently says what Milton would like to say but does not dare, and despite his appearance no one could describe him as 'nice'. Milton calls him a 'film maker' and says he is very good

* Actually she had turned thirty in June.
** b.1931. With his older brother Albert he went on to make a number of acclaimed documentary films (*Salesman*, *Gimme Shelter*, *Grey Gardens* etc.).

in his own right. But he spends most of his time running errands (like me) and chasing girls. He is flippant but cheerful. He is always playing with Josh, which gives Amy a break, and he makes Amy laugh, which makes me jealous, I'm not sure why. He told me that Milton orders the pills for MM from Amy's doctor in New York. There are 'uppers' for when she is down, and 'downers' for when she cannot relax. I gather that in America you can buy any pill you want. Don't they realise that nature has already worked out how to keep you balanced without uppers and downers? I know they think MM is a special case, and I suppose she does have unnatural pressures and demands. But now she is like a see-saw, forever being pushed up or down and never level. In the end she will loop the loop like her mum.

FRIDAY, 28 SEPTEMBER

More hall but no Monroe. Hedda called at about ten to say she wasn't well again. Plod had already phoned to tell me that there was no sign of life at 8.30 and I had warned SLO. Milton was caught unawares, and SLO despatched him to see if a doctor had been called, or was contemplated.

There is still plenty we can do without MM. After lunch we did the shot of the Grand Duke's arrival at the Embassy, just as Elsie has decided to walk out. She turns to the front door to leave, which we have already shot, and then we cut to the back of her head. The big doors open, she curtseys and her head disappears downwards to reveal SLO's grinning face.

'Good evening,' he says. 'How kind of you to come at such short notice.'

He really looked most alarming with his monocle and his patent leather hair, but he did several 'takes', until he was absolutely happy with this ghastly appearance. In MM's absence we did the shot with MM's stand-in bobbing up and down in one of MM's precious wigs. She was thrilled to be 'understudy-ing' MM even if one couldn't see her face, and she has got over her anger with me.

All this made it clear that I had somehow to make it up with Jack. By pure luck I heard him talking enthusiastically about the Turner paintings in the Tate Gallery. He was sitting in a little circle of admirers – Carmen, Tony, Denys and Co – while he waited for the gaffer to do his bidding. I was standing (3rd Ast Dirs never sit, remember) on the edge of the circle, and I butted in.

'My father owns one of those paintings,' I said.

'No,' said Jack kindly, 'these are all in the Tate Gallery, and the ones I am talking about are very big.'

'Well, my father has the only one in the world outside the Tate,' I replied. 'Somehow it escaped and my father bought it nine years ago. It's hanging in the drawing room.' Jack had to look at me again. 'The drawing room' probably wasn't a concept he associated with 3rd Ast Dirs. They are meant to talk about the lounge. I'm sure that in his nice, easy-going way it has never occurred to him that I was of any particular significance (i.e. the son of friends of SLO and Vivien etc.). Why should it? I've never looked at the stand-ins like that, and I see them every day just as Jack sees me. But now he was curious. (Snob-bishness, too, is a sympathetic human failing.)

'Is your father a collector, then?' he asked, prepared to be dealing with a lunatic.

'Yes, he is. He's an art historian actually.'

Jack's mind did a rapid search of his memory. Colin Clark?? 'Your father isn't Sir Kenneth Clark, is he?'

'Yes, he is.' No reaction from the crew. Carmen already knew this but none of the others had ever heard of art historians, let alone Sir Kenneth Clark. Jack is an artist with light who also aspires to be an artist with paint. Jack nearly jumped out of Jack's skin with excitement.

'Oh, how wonderful. I admire your father very much. I'd love to meet him and discuss painting with him. In fact he owns the picture I admire most in the world – the nude portrait Renoir did of his wife on their honeymoon.'

I was just warming up. 'Perhaps you and Mrs Cardiff would like to come down to the country one weekend. You could meet my parents and see the Renoir and the other pictures.' All this was out of the MM stand-in's earshot. (When you wield such flagrant power, you must be merciful!)

'Oh, that would be fantastic. I'll tell Julie' – for thus Mrs C is called – 'She will be thrilled. Perhaps we could drive down. It is in Kent isn't it?' Yes, and it's a castle as I'm sure you know, but I didn't say that.

'I'm going down this weekend and I'll arrange it,' I said. 'I'm sure my parents would be flattered to meet you both.'

Victory over stand-in complete. Indeed Jack went round telling everyone, whether they had heard of Sir Kenneth Clark or not. SLO took it calmly. 'You'll love K and Jane. Gorgeous house, too,' he said without taking much notice. Poor man has other problems right now. But I'm very happy. Jack is a nice, interesting and enthusiastic man and I'm sure my parents will like him and his wife.

Mr P came into the studio at the end of the day, delightfully gloomy as ever. He has already had to put his Number 2 cross-plot into effect, but for some reason he blames AM and not MM. The demand for a Jaguar was seen as a last straw. He also has suspicions that Paula Strasberg is fleecing us and that Milton is fleecing MM.

'So who do you trust?' I asked.

'No one, Colin – including you.' Grin, grin.

MONDAY, 1 OCTOBER

MM had been told she need not come in today or tomorrow. It's very doubtful if she would have turned up anyway. Once the word 'doctor' has been mentioned, it usually takes three days for her to recover her stamina and her will power.

We have two days in the Foreign Office set, which has been built in Studio A. It needs its own studio because film we shot on location two weeks ago is projected onto a screen outside the windows, to look as if the carriages are going trotting by in the background. We filmed the coaches from the actual Foreign Secretary's office, looking down on the road round St James's Park. The carriages were so far away that we used the stand-ins, dressed in the stars' costumes. We will film the stars themselves in close-up later, in the studio.

The BP* needs a long throw and powerful arc lamps. These are noisy. They hiss away and get extremely hot. If you even glimpse one straight on you are blind for half an hour. So they have to be quite far from the camera and the microphone. Setting them up is a complicated business, and so is the art of balancing the light between the actors in the room and the light projected on the screen behind them. There were considerable delays while adjustments were made. Two totally competent actors (Dicky Wattis and David Horne) went through their lines again and again. Sounds familiar? Of course this is what happens every day, but for once it was not MM's fault. It was a piece of antiquated lighting equipment, which makes a pretty unconvincing picture at the end of the day. Does anyone complain? Not a soul. Just because the antiquated lighting equipment didn't flounce off to a mobile dressing room, shaking its fingers? Technical matters, and especially lighting matters, are

* i.e. back projection.

above criticism – out of bounds. If you dare question what is going on you get dark looks, scowls and murmurs of union displeasure. It is as if we were ruled by some secret society, with its own rules into which we must never enquire. And indeed that is true. The Electricians' Union is above any question or criticism, yet it can bring the whole studio to a halt at a moment's notice. Everyone behaves as if technical mysteries are so mysterious that only technicians can understand them. Absolute nonsense! It is all simple and basic. All this mystery is just to hide laziness and incompetence, to make sure that three men are hired to do the job of one. The art of acting is far more mysterious, yet every technician feels free to criticise MM. They damn her every time she has an attack of nerves, as if it was *she* who was lazy and incompetent. It is MM who really lights up the screen, and not some engineers fiddling with switches. But of course I could never say this in public, not even to David.

TUESDAY, 2 OCTOBER

More Foreign Office. The scene seems dry as dust. This is partly intentional – the stuffy old Foreign Office having to cope with exotic Balkan Grand Dukes. But the main problem is that the scene does not contain MM. SLO playing Oedipus and Hamlet simultaneously wouldn't generate as much excitement as MM on screen. Drugged, confused, frightened, late, vague, maddening as she can be, she changes any scene from night to day. Without her, we are all just technicians arguing about our unimportant little problems. Even dear Dicky W can only add to a scene, not create one.

There is no denying that MM has problems. She is herself one gigantic problem. But she is also the solution! As long as she can get to the studio and walk onto the set, it is worth everything to film her. This plump, blonde(?) young lady with the big eyes is certainly very hard to control. Right now she is almost too much for a young, smart producer (Milton), a top playwright and intellectual (AM), America's foremost dramatic coaching couple (the Strasbergs) and England's best actor/director (SLO). MM is just a force of nature. That is sort of wonderful for us, to watch and be associated with, but it must be very uncomfortable for her. I wonder if Garbo was like this, or Chaplin. Vivien is a force of nature too, but she is so formidably intelligent that, to some extent, she can control it. MM does not have that power – and even Vivien can lose it sometimes, come to think of it.

WEDNESDAY, 3 OCTOBER

Plod called first thing. Lee Strasberg had arrived yesterday from New York, to take personal charge of MM's performance in the film. MM wasn't coming in today, but Lee Strasberg was!

'Well done, Plod.' Spies are useful. Even half an hour's warning is better than total surprise. I ran to SLO's dressing room with the news.

Predictably SLO exploded. 'Paula's bad enough. I'm the f—ing director of this f—ing film. Call Milton. I'm the f—ing producer too. I won't allow Lee Strasberg on the set. Call the studio police, and have him stopped at the gate. F— him.'

I had already squeezed in a call to Tibbs, and Milton was on his way.

'Send him in here as soon as he arrives. He can go to the main gate and explain. Why is Lee here, for Christ's sake?'

Me: 'Perhaps MM has asked him to come.'

'Well she can't have him, at least not in my studio.'

This was not the moment to remind him that MM was an equal partner.

'We are only halfway through this f—ing movie. This will

make it impossible to finish. I can't direct with so many people interfering' etc., until Milton arrived.

'Milton, dear boy, this is a very expensive film we are making. We aren't a bunch of psychoanalysts trying to sort out Marilyn's mental health. WE ARE MAKING A FILM. I can't work with Lee Strasberg on the set. I can't even work with Paula Strasberg on the set. We agreed she would stay in Marilyn's dressing room, if you remember. I am the only director allowed on the set. Understood?' Milton shrugged gloomily. 'Well, dear boy, run along and explain that to Lee. He'll be arriving at the main gate any minute – COLIN!'

'Yes, Sir Laurence.'

'Oh, there you are.' I'd been making myself as small as possible about three feet away in the same room. 'Go and get Jack and Tony and David. We'll plan the day without Marilyn. It's just as well she isn't coming in. Then Lee can't interfere.'

I rushed off. I have to be very careful with these messages. It is *not* a good idea to arrive on the set, out of breath and clearly in possession of important news no one else has. I have to sidle up to each recipient in turn, tell them the message as if it was specially sent to them alone by SLO. Each one says: 'Have you told Jack? or David? or Tony?' and I indicate that they will be next on the list, even if I've already told them. Only when all of them know can I dash over to Dicky and Paul and burst out with the latest gossip.

Today we have a new set in Studio B – a small sitting room of the Embassy, downstairs, leading off the Grand Hall. It has an attractive garden at the rear, completely false, of course, with a summer house. There was a lot of preparation going on. Carmen and Dario like to keep adding things up to the last minute, thereby driving Elaine crazy. Elaine actually never loses her cool manner (but she does get very severe).

By lunchtime SLO and Tony B were quite cheerful. Milton had warned Lee, and Lee had been upset but contrite. He had

rushed across the Atlantic at MM and Paula's frantic bidding
only to realise, in the cold light of an English October morning,
that there is no magic wand where MM is concerned. The truth
is that MM is unhappy here. She no longer thinks that the film
will transform her career from dumb blonde to serious actress
(as if . . .). She doesn't trust SLO, or think that she can learn
anything from him (this is probably true). She has mixed feelings about Milton, and suspects his motives (wrongly I think).
She is not even that happy with AM and looks as if she thinks
he isn't really in love with her (also probably true). She does
not even know what she does want, so how can Lee give it to
her? Lee is a really clever man. I met him outside the star
entrance and we had a long chat while he was waiting for the car
(which had immediately returned to Parkside, like a brainless
homing pigeon). I asked him about Susie and told him what a
fan of hers I was. (She came over with him and is staying at
the Dorchester.)

I said if he could just persuade MM to finish the film, which
is halfway through, then everyone could relax and be happy
again. Luckily he agreed. Seven more weeks of hard work
seems a lot, but he is sure MM will do it. He is only staying
two nights, but Susie is staying two weeks, so I am sure to
meet her. (Currently one of my life's ambitions!) I think Lee's
visit has been 'cathartic' and may actually help quite a lot. It
has allowed everyone to put their cards on the table. He is one
of the few intelligent people who can get through to MM, and
he doesn't have an axe to grind. We'll see.

THURSDAY, 4 OCTOBER

MM did come in this morning, and quite bright and cheerful
she was, if a little forced. So far so good. She always likes a
new set too. Today we were out in the garden, with Jeremy
whom she still (just) gets on with, so we were all full of fresh

hope. The garden has a nice sunny feel to it when the lights are on, but to achieve this effect means more light than usual and therefore more heat. MM had to wear the raincoat over her dress in these scenes, and that meant she perspired a lot, and had to change clothes a lot,* with consequent delays. Nothing is easy in the film business. But MM's nerve held. Jeremy was as charming as usual and SLO was in a more confident mood. He felt he had achieved a victory over the Strasbergs, and this he badly needed. He became more avuncular with MM, and not so tense and tetchy, which I am sure she appreciated.

After lunch, who should appear but Susan Strasberg. I have always been looking forward to meeting her more than meeting MM. Even seeing MM in the nude had left me cold – well not exactly cold, to be honest, but not in love. But Susie had stolen my heart, in her movie. Susie is not exactly pretty, but she is luminously beautiful. She has huge brown eyes, a very full mouth with a wide grin, and skin so pale that it is almost translucent. She arrived on the set with Paula, looking like a real little star. Luckily Paula and I have always got along – I've made sure of that – and I've made no secret of my admiration for Lee, so I got a very good introduction: 'This is Colin, who has been so helpful. He's the son of the Lord, Kenneth Clark.' (Americans never understand English titles.) I was completely tongue-tied and could only gulp, as usual. Susie was enchanting.

'I love film studios. Do show me round. Marilyn won't be ready for ages.' (True.)

The film crew watched in amazement as their 3rd Ast Dir gulped off into the distance with this ravishing little creature. In fact she was so nice to me that by the end of the day I had bucked up courage to ask her to have dinner with me, and been invited to come to the Dorchester next Tuesday evening.

Having said all this, I have to admit that Susie is out of my

---

* Bumble Dawson had provided three identical white dresses.

league. She's a Star. She's used to mixing with Stars, like William Holden, and although she is no older than me (or younger?*), I can only relate to her the way I do to Vivien. Adoration and devotion, but embraces are unthinkable. Even so, I am very excited. I can dream of it even if I can't think of it.

Jack and Mrs C are invited for the night at Saltwood this weekend, so I will drive down there immediately after work tomorrow.

RUNNYMEDE, SUNDAY, 7 OCTOBER

I got to Saltwood too late for dinner on Friday night and had to go to the pub for sausage rolls. The Castle Arms is not to be recommended for its food, but if I asked for a late supper at home the servants would all give notice. M and D were very sweet and understanding about the Cardiffs' visit. Papa even said that he had heard of Jack (from *The Red Shoes*) and was looking forward to meeting him. When they arrived on Saturday at noon, they were immediately taken round the garden by Mama. Not many flowers, but the roses are pretty on a good second showing. It was sunny and the castle always looks impressive in the autumn. Jack and Mrs C are really charming. They were both very appreciative and Mama was delighted. Then we had drinks in the drawing room and Jack waxed lyrical about the Renoir until lunch. I could see Mrs C was more taken with the idea of our own cook and butler. M and D, who usually only have guests as sophisticated as themselves, enjoyed the visit thoroughly. In the afternoon, I took the Cardiffs over to Canterbury, which they had not seen. Then in the evening Papa took Jack round the other pictures and over to the Great Hall, while Mama had a good heart to heart with Mrs C. (I dread to

* In fact she was only eighteen. She had appeared with William Holden in *Picnic*.

think what she told her about me!) After dinner, when Papa had announced 'Bed for all' and started turning off the lights, I held Jack back and we both stayed in the small library for a whisky and soda. Jack was extremely mellow and we had a long chat about work. Naturally he is worried. He can see that MM is driving SLO nuts, and this is having a bad effect on the production as a whole. This is a very important film for him.

Then Jack told me a secret. Evidently, a couple of weeks after filming started, MM found an open notebook on AM's desk at Parkside. In it, AM had written some pretty bad stuff about MM – how disappointed he was by her etc. MM had been absolutely shattered. No wonder she took pills and came on set as Ophelia instead of Elsie Marina. I guessed that AM didn't love her enough. Whatever he felt, he shouldn't have written it down and left it for MM to discover like that. Jack had comforted MM as best he could.

Jack told me this to show how deeply he was in MM's confidence. I wish she could have told SLO. It might have made it easier for him to understand her behaviour. But now it is definitely too late. If SLO heard what AM had written he would just say 'She's a disappointment to me too!'

Nevertheless I did ask Jack to share everything with me in the future. I am the only person who picks up all the little bits of information and can put it to SLO when I know he will listen. If he explodes at me it doesn't matter. He never stays angry for long. Of course I will never tell SLO anything unless Jack agrees, but at least he and I can talk over the problems. I only have SLO's interests at heart. Jack is more concerned with the film, but it is SLO's film, so we all have the same purpose in the end. Jack and I went to bed firm friends and that must be a good thing.

When I got back here, Tony broke it to me that he and Anne are giving up this house in two weeks' time. Somehow I had assumed that they had it for the duration of the film, but they don't want the responsibility in the winter. I can't blame them.

They have been wonderfully tolerant of me. I have used their house like a hotel – and I haven't shown them enough gratitude. Evidently Anne's grown-up son (Ned, I think) is coming back, and they have to be in London. I must find somewhere else round here. I could not do this job if I had to commute from the West End.

MONDAY, 8 OCTOBER

MM arrived quite early this morning and completed a long scene with SLO before lunch! In fairness to her, I must record that she did it well and was really quite professional. This was partly due to her being clear in the head for a change, and partly due to this bit of script being much more suitable to her talents – also for a change. I've always thought that this was a lousy vehicle for MM as well as for SLO.

Rattigan couldn't write the menu on a fish and chip shop blackboard. *The Prince and the Showgirl* is all so light, it's like a sort of 'in-joke'. If it's Larry or Vivien in the theatre, the audience can join in. But for the film-going public? I very much doubt it.

Today MM had something she could get her teeth into. She had to tease, and she had to control. When the Grand Duke lost patience, and swore in German, she had to slap her hand on the table and cry: 'Well done. That's the best yet!' She clearly enjoyed it and it showed.

SLO thinks that all the top stars should be able to act anything. Actually everyone else in the film has been carefully chosen to match their roles – Dicky W and Dame S are obvious examples. Did he ever think if this was the *right* role for MM? Did Milton? Was MM consulted on that, or did they all think that as MM was an 'actress', she could easily play a song and dance girl? That is what she is acting, of course, but what she is *meant* to act is Elsie Marina as created by Rattigan. Where her concept and Rattigan's concept don't fit together the friction causes her (and us) pain. I suppose they all leapt at the chance of Olivier and Monroe in the same film, and then slotted in a script that seemed suitable. There were similar-ish roles for SLO and MM, and only four major sets so it looked quite cheap to make. Olivier also knew exactly how to play it and on whom he could rely to make it work. Roger, Bumble, Tony, and Rattigan himself, Billy Chappell and Addinsell. But did MM read the script and think 'This is me' or 'I can impersonate this girl' or 'I have a deep feeling for this character and long to portray her on film' or indeed anything at all? Whenever there is a scene which suits her mood, she can do more than we expect. Even in the love scene this afternoon, she surprised us by how well she performed. But if she had spent a few days going through the script before we started with a really sympathetic director, things might be very different now. Those rehearsals were really only for her. The other actors don't need them. It was a smoke screen put up so she wouldn't feel singled out. But in the event, and because the others were so professional, she was made to feel uncomfortable, and the rehearsals had the opposite effect to that intended. It's easy to be wise after the event, but I don't think SLO *thought* enough!

TUESDAY, 9 OCTOBER

A series of 'tender' scenes between SLO and MM made for a gradual deterioration of MM's morale and confidence level, and a consequent shortening of SLO's fuse. MM doesn't seem to mind the actual kiss as much as SLO does. It was shot over SLO's shoulder, to favour MM, and SLO does not actually kiss her lips. In all the embraces, he just kisses her between the lips and her chin. (This is a theatrical trick, I suppose. SLO is not the first leading man who cannot stand his leading lady!) MM has probably had more experience of being kissed by someone she doesn't like, or even doesn't know. But SLO gets completely rigid, as if it is agony for him to get so close to her. His performance has been too severe, for my taste, all through the movie. I'm sure royalty were like that in 1911, autocratic and self-centred, but this is a Fairy Story, for heaven's sake, not a historical drama.

I had a long discussion about this with Susie S tonight. She invited me to the Dorchester and when I got to her room, she announced that she didn't want to go out for dinner, and we would eat there. This sounds like a cue for romance, but alas it was not. Susie is a beautiful person – intelligent, sensitive, full of life and fun, but her heart is more mature than mine. It has probably been broken a few times already, and it works on a different level. So we ordered dinner (the waiter was incredibly rude; so much for the Dorchester) and chatted about the film, and her parents, and all the problems in between. Susie has great insight into MM. She is nearer to MM's age than the rest of them, and must face many similar challenges. The two 'girls' obviously get on very well. Of course Susie doesn't see the desire for control in her own Mum that drives AM and Milton to distraction. The trouble is that MM simply cries out for someone to control her, and no one can resist trying to do so. She dumps her problems in Paula's lap, and then while the wretched woman is trying to sort them out, MM goes and dumps them on someone else, and they start working on them, and so on.

Susie says that Paula is going back to NYC in a week. Her permit to stay in England will expire soon, and anyway she needs a break. Then all MM's problems will be our problems. Hedda is going back too, but she has never been much help. Susie has promised to come down to Saltwood for the night next Saturday. I feel thrilled. I know I can't remotely possess her but I still can't resist her charm. I stayed up too late tonight but I'm happy. It's my 24th birthday. I didn't tell Susie, though. I want her to think I'm older.

WEDNESDAY, 10 OCTOBER

MM was very troubled today. She had the greatest difficulty remembering even the simplest line – again. We were shooting the continuation of the farewell scene and there were some long takes.

'Oh dear. This time it is up to me to be grown up' gave her a lot of difficulty. She got it in her head that the scene was tragic, and it really isn't written that way.

At one stage, she had to ask: 'Poor darling, do you feel terribly disconcerted?' This was said tenderly but lightly by Vivien in the play. It is a sort of Rattigan joke because 'disconcerted' is one of the Grand Duke's favourite words. Poor MM could not get the point. Because she wasn't allowed to play it as a tragedy, she simply failed to remember it. Her frantic hesitation, as she searched her memory and grabbed the line out of the air, may look like passion. We will see at rushes tomorrow, but it was the best we could get.

THURSDAY, 11 OCTOBER

Dame Sybil back, punctual as ever despite her play. It is pitch dark at 6.45 a.m. now and very cold, but the red scarf is still all I need over my jacket.

Dame S had a great scene, sweeping in to the downstairs sitting room, giving MM a photograph and a medal and lots of advice before sweeping out again, with Dicky Wattis and the ladies-in-waiting in her wake. Her line 'You may kiss me, my dear' reminded me of Papa's story about Empress Eugenie in Menton.* MM looked as surprised as Papa had been. I think she'd forgotten about that bit, as she had no line to speak, but she managed it well. She still responds to Dame S's uncomplicated warmth of character. After lunch we did Elsie Marina's farewell to the Grand Duke in the hall. She is standing alone in the doorway of the sitting room, and she looked a forlorn figure. I wish we could have ended the filming then. It would have made a nice memory. But there is still a long way to go. The coaches, the Abbey, the Grand Ball and the theatre, not to speak of the exteriors on the 'lot'.

At least I have found somewhere to live. It is just a room over the pub a couple of miles from here, but I can get supper there too. They've asked if I can help behind the bar! Free beer?

FRIDAY, 12 OCTOBER

There are two separate sets of scenes in the coaches – each with a back-projection screen to make them look as if they were going along the road. The first were done in the morning, while MM was getting ready. SLO, Dame S, Jeremy and the

* In 1911, when my father was eight, he met Empress Eugenie in Menton. She invited him to kiss her, but since he had never kissed anyone in his life, including his parents, he turned and fled.

Ambassador (who only appears once again and never speaks, poor man) took turns to feature in close-ups which will fit into the stuff we shot outside the Foreign Office. The coach party salute and bow gravely to non-existent passers-by, but of course they do not speak. No sound always makes for a very easy shoot, even though we all stay quiet as mice. It means that Mitch doesn't have to fuss where his boom can go, without it casting a shadow on the stars. Then the BP film was changed from St James's Park to the crowded stands of cheering people on the way to the Coronation. In squeezed Dame S and MM on one side, SLO and Dicky opposite them, prepared to be rocked gently up and down and cued to react as ordered. Dame S had a funny speech about her last coronation: 'Happily no fatalities – except in the crowd' – turning to wave to them. MM had to 'silent act', or react, a lot, which is not her 'forte'.

I'm not surprised she was a little hysterical. She went to the first night of AM's play – *A View from the Bridge* – last night and she must be exhausted. The papers are full of her 'low-cut crimson dress'. Evidently it brought the house down more than the play. Plod said AM didn't mind a bit. His ego is impregnable.

I dined this evening with Al at the club. Quite a relief to feel civilised again. Al takes a pretty jaundiced view of 'Showbiz' and is not too sympathetic when I describe my lack of love life either. 'You should be tougher, old boy.'

I know he is right. He is wonderful company, much cleverer than I am, but that's what's great. Talking of unsuccessful love life, I am driving Susie down to Saltwood tomorrow morning. At least I have the new Lancia Aurelia GT to take her in, but I don't expect she'll notice.

The Prince, the Showgirl and Me

CARPENTERS' ARMS, SUNDAY, 14 OCTOBER

Susie was a magical weekend guest. She chattered away merrily on the drive and enchanted Mama and Papa as soon as she arrived. She is a good talker but also a very good listener, and there is nothing Papa likes more than a pretty girl who listens.

After lunch I invited her for a walk along 'the white cliffs of Dover' in the sunshine. As we were whizzing in to Folkestone an elderly car in front of us pulled over to the right, signalled a right turn by hand and indicator and then turned sharply left. Only the Lancia brakes saved me from the dubious distinction of putting Hollywood's most promising actress straight through the windshield. Even so, we banged the left side of the other car. A policeman on a motorbike actually witnessed the whole event from the other side of the road and came over. It turned out that the combined age of the four occupants in the other car was over 320, and the whole thing quickly developed into a farce. The driver, who was not the youngest, started to explain to the policeman. 'I'm just a silly old fool,' he said. The policeman had his crash helmet on and misheard. 'Who are you calling a fool?' he asked menacingly. But the driver was deaf too and persisted. Cross purposes set in all over the place, and Susie and I quickly left before we got complete giggles. But up on the cliff, Susie suddenly went silent and preoccupied, and we hardly spoke until we got back to the castle. Perhaps it was the shock.*

She recovered during dinner, and by the time I dropped her back to the Dorchester this evening we were the firmest of friends. I do hope to see her again, but I somehow doubt it.

* I later learned that Susan had just been jilted by Richard Burton, who had been her lover. She wrote in her autobiography that she had been thinking about jumping off the cliff. Quite a compliment to my company!

She will marry some super star and that will be that. Is there nothing for me between a little Wdg and a Hollywood star?

MONDAY, 15 OCTOBER

The coach was a lot easier to work with when it just sat on rockers in front of a BP screen. As soon as horses were attached it became unpredictable, no matter how many grooms were standing by. We started the day with it actually in the studio, outside the front door of the Embassy. SLO, MM, Dame S and Dicky had to walk out of the hall and get into it, on their way to the Abbey. A seedy bunch of extras stood around outside, hiding the fact that Belgrave Square was missing. There was no dialogue, so getting into the coach was not much problem, but each time it set off, it was with a mighty lurch.

This did not look good, so the coach had to be backed up, and everyone extricated before we could try again. Tony B was directing – since SLO was in the blooming thing – and he could not be satisfied. These repeated neck-snapping departures were quite trying on the nerves of the passengers, and also on their costumes, wigs, monocles etc. In the end, SLO had had enough. 'Print the bloody lot,' he said. 'We'll choose the best at rushes. One of them seemed OK to me.' Tony pretended to be angry, but he was secretly relieved. He can never be angry with 'Laurence' for more than 10 seconds, anyway.

After lunch, we took the coach and the stars and about 150 extras onto a windy 'lot' to do a little trotting about. It was extremely hard for Jack to light, even with arc lights. It isn't meant to be sunny, after all. They went under a false Admiralty Arch with MM getting very excited and Dicky W looking nervous (real-life nervous). Then they reached the theatre in which Elsie Marina was performing. In front of it was a stand, packed with the cast of Elsie's musical comedy, *The Coconut Girl*. Tomorrow this group will have dialogue, but for today they only had to cheer wildly, toot horns and wave flags. They are a lovely bunch of actors and actresses, very good hearted and jolly, despite the weather and the delays. They know they aren't at the centre of the film but this doesn't seem to worry them a bit. For them, any work is better than nothing. I hope MM doesn't have to learn this hard lesson one day.

TUESDAY, 16 OCTOBER

No more coach and horses and no more MM either. She had a day off. The weather is cold and grey so we had arc lights on the lot again. At least it didn't rain. One never films in the rain, David tells me. 'Film rain' is always carefully directed from a special hose pipe. But the lack of rain clouds worried Jack Harris. There is no pleasing a film editor!

The theatre cast did their dialogue in medium shot, so very few extras were involved. Jean Kent* is 'the star' and she looks lovely. I fancied her like mad when I was a teenager and she was a heroine of B movies. Gladys Henson** is the dresser, and she reminds me of the little Wdg's boss (who now disapproves of me so much). There are three super girls who play MM's special friends – Vera Day is very cute and cockney, Gillian Owen is dark and quiet, and Daphne Anderson is just lovely. She has generous smiling eyes and a wide mouth – the sort of big-sister friend any actress would dream of having in real life. She shares 'digs' with Elsie Marina and there will be a scene there later. And of course they all feature in the back-stage action, which we will film last of all. For now, Daphne has a trumpet which she blows mightily to catch MM's attention. (It doesn't really make any noise at all. The 'toots' will be added

---

* b.1921. Her many films – not all of them 'B's – included *Fanny by Gaslight*, *The Wicked Lady*, *The Rake's Progress* and Rattigan's *The Browning Version*.
** (1897–1983). Irish actress who specialised in warm-hearted maternal characters.

later.) Then we 'shot' the girls on the pavement outside the Embassy, waving and tooting again. Beside them was the barrel organ which is meant to be making the music which Elsie is dancing to when Jeremy comes into the purple room. Naturally, it too doesn't make a sound. My goodness, what a long time ago that purple room seems.

Incidentally we saw the rushes of our efforts yesterday and the coach does seem to jerk mightily on departure every time. It is always doubtful when you insert a note of reality into a fairy story but I think it will work. In fact it looked quite amusing to me, if not to Tony.

WEDNESDAY, 17 OCTOBER

Paula has gone back to NYC, taking Susie with her. This is seen as a great victory by the anti-Paula brigade but it is bound to put an added strain on MM, and indeed on AM. Luckily, it coincided with her getting very good reviews in all the papers for her latest film, *Bus Stop.* Josh Logan, the director, told a different story, but as usual the only thing that matters with a film is the final result. So MM was full of the joys of spring on a cold grey morning. Just as well. We are still on the lot, and this scene follows her dance. She was happy when she did the dance, so she has to be happy now. And that isn't easy when you are perched up behind a fake window in a long white evening dress. There wasn't any serious dialogue to remember. The first time she looks out of the window – or through it, since it is out of doors, there is only a crowd of extras beneath. The second time she sees her friends and waves. Then she has to hush them, as she pretends that she is listening to Jeremy on the phone. This was a little hard for her. 'Listening Intently' does not conjure up any particular expression. MM chose anxiety – not a difficult one for her to choose, given the circumstances. Then Elsie moves out onto the broad balcony over the

front door, to reassure her friends and talk about the Grand
Duke. The final shot was of the Grand Duke, standing in front
of another fake window reacting to her description of him. In
these window shots, SLO always exaggerates and stands too
close to the edge – both of the window frame and the camera
frame. I know he wants the audience to be sure to see MM in
the background, but it looks artificial. He did just the same in
the purple room, but if Tony doesn't see it there is certainly
nothing I can say.

THURSDAY, 18 OCTOBER

We are back in the studio to film the interior of Westminster
Abbey. Roger has built two sides of the nave with an arch in
between. As usual with film sets, when you first see it you can't
believe it will work, but it always does. The angles have been
worked out long in advance. SLO and Dame S are on one side
of the Abbey, and the arch, and MM sits next to Dicky W on
the other, but they can see one another. By now we all assume
MM will be late (I wish we'd done that from the beginning),
so we started with Dame S and SLO, sitting among a group
of the most distinguished-looking extras we could find. These
were dressed as other minor royalty and ambassadors and they
looked pretty good. Everyone stood up and bowed as a row
of even more elderly extras trooped past, dressed as 'serjeants
at arms' or whatever, escorting the royal couple. Rightly King
George V and Queen Mary were left to the imagination! When
MM arrived, we did the same procedure with her and Dicky.
MM looked suitably awed and was on best behaviour. She's
always more relaxed when there is no dialogue (who isn't?).
She had a very pretty headdress and necklace on which the
Queen Mum (Dame S) had lent her earlier on.

After his usual conference with SLO, Milton asked me to go
back with him to Tibbs. He and Amy then invited me to move

in to the spare room at Tibbs and stay for the rest of the movie.
I was overwhelmed.

'When?' was all I could say.

'Tonight if you want to.' It's true that I don't have much
luggage, but I must say goodbye properly to my friends at the
pub so I am back here for another couple of nights.

'Can I come on Saturday afternoon?'

'Whenever you like.' That open hospitality, with no strings
attached, is absolutely the best side of the American character.
Milton and Amy have always been so easy-going and friendly
and I am absolutely thrilled. I suddenly realise how lonely life
has been here. Now I feel back in the family again.

FRIDAY, 19 OCTOBER

Today was MM's big day. At last she really had to act in a
'method' way. She had a chance to put all she had learned from
Lee Strasberg into practice. No song and dance, no flippant
chat. She had to feel emotions and convey them to the camera
with nothing to help her other than her own face. She is in the
Abbey; she is in close-up; she is in the midst of a solemn and
historic occasion. The Monarch of England is being crowned.
Now that is pretty strong stuff for a showgirl. Of course to act
in a conventional SLO way would have been easier. But MM
had been determined to do something the 'method' way or bust
in the attempt. The problem is that with the crew all round –
and there are often as many as 60 people behind the camera*
– it is very hard to sit and *feel* anything. It must be easier to
pretend you feel them, but that would be cheating! Elsie was
supposed to be so overcome with the drama of it all that tears
spring to her eyes. Evidently MM has done the tears trick in
previous movies, and she is rather proud of the achievement,

---

* Nowadays it would be more like three hundred.

so she had told SLO that it would be no problem. She had been powerfully briefed by Paula before she left. 'Think of Frank Sinatra. Think of Coca-Cola,' Paula had said. (I swear that is a direct quote.) But in the event, poor MM could not manage to squeeze a single tear. Loud Handel ('Zadok the Priest'??, I think), played on a tape in the studio, meant nothing to her. (Why should it?) Her lips parted and quivered and she seemed to go into a trance. The camera rolled away a lot of very expensive film, but no tears came. Glycerine was produced to make fake tears but she refused it. She flushed an un-makeupable rash and we all settled down to wait some more – while she went back to her dressing room.

I fancy she had a couple of glasses of champagne to steady the nerves, but for whatever reason, when she came back to the set, a real tear did indeed trickle down her cheek. A triumph for the Actors' Studio indeed, but glycerine would have been much quicker!

This is my last night in the pub. They were all very kind and gave me a jolly evening. Funnily enough I found that I have drunk much less in the evenings than I usually do. Perhaps after the film is over, I should get a job working behind a bar instead of sitting in front of it!

TIBBS FARM, SUNDAY, 21 OCTOBER

It is simply great to be at Tibbs. What luxury after the pub, and even dear Runnymede. There is nothing like deep pile Wilton underfoot in the bathroom. Milton and Amy run an open house, with drink and food always available. Milton's assistant David Maysles is very 'laid back' and easy-going. I suppose he and I are a bit too alike to be friends. He is to Milton what I am to SLO, and so we both know what makes the other tick, and how much ambition lurks beneath the surface. David has an incredibly pretty girl friend, an English actress called June Thorburn.* (There he is definitely one up on me.) Both of us are 'gofers' for now, and no gofer likes gofering in front of another gofer, which makes us wary of each other. In his case, he is forever running down to the shops (on a motorscooter) to get Milton and Amy fresh supplies. I think Amy is taking Josh back to USA soon, and then life will get even more relaxed. There is only one problem. It is going to be very difficult to go up to bed at 9.30 p.m. I have found that if I want seven hours' sleep, from 10.30 p.m. to 5.30 a.m., I have to be in my room by 9.45 p.m. I need the time to write this diary, and to compose myself. Milton likes to start to eat dinner at 9 p.m. One thing is certain, I still have to be at Pinewood by 6.40 a.m. each morning if I want to keep my job.

MONDAY, 22 OCTOBER

Plod called up, early, to say that a new 'shrink' had arrived from the USA to see MM, a Doctor Hohenberg I think. Just what MM needs – another daft piece of advice from someone with instant solutions! He** may hold her hand and calm her down temporarily but it would take years to cure her problems permanently. His arrival definitely means MM will not be in today.

We have moved into the Grand Ballroom set. SLO and Dicky had a nice scene with Maxine Audley.*** Maxine is Lady Sunningdale, an old girl friend of the Grand Duke's. (Her name is a typical 'in joke' of Rattigan's. He lives in Wentworth, which is just down the road from Sunningdale, and people who live in Wentworth look down on Sunningdale.) The Grand Duke

---

* (1931–67). Her films included *The Pickwick Papers*, *The Cruel Sea*, *Tom Thumb*.
** Actually Dr Hohenberg was a she.
*** (1923–92). Distinguished stage actress whose occasional film appearances included *The Barretts of Wimpole Street*, *Our Man in Havana*, *The Trials of Oscar Wilde*. She was a great friend of Vivien Leigh.

is setting up a date for later that evening, because Elsie Marina had passed out on him the night before. She had drunk 'an amount of vodka which, in Carpathia, you would add to the morning milk of a two-year-old child' – in reality about six glasses, plus champagne. Naturally SLO and Dicky and Maxine played the scene impeccably. They have all acted together many times. It was only the 'extras' and the lights which needed attention. Maxine used to be a great beauty on stage. She is still very handsome (and sexy), but compared to MM she looks tired. SLO and Jeremy have very fine matching white uniforms, with red sashes. A ball scene really brings out the best in Bumble (and Cecil Beaton), and the ladies' dresses are equally sumptuous.

My main task was to look after the horde of extras, mostly members of old-time dancing clubs, who will fill the ballroom tomorrow. They have to be carefully shepherded between wardrobe, where their costumes are fitted, to dance rehearsals with Billy Chappell. Unlike regular FAA extras, they must not be yelled at and ordered around. Our regular extras are still here, of course, as guests and servants, and anyone else who doesn't speak or dance. They will all be on camera tomorrow. It is going to be a hectic week. At least Milton had no one to dinner tonight so I could slink up here early with a sandwich from the 'fridge'.

TUESDAY, 23 OCTOBER

The dancers looked fabulous as they swirled round the studio floor. There are real crystal chandeliers, and Roger has included a magnificent carpeted staircase with a full orchestra at the bottom of it. Roger, Carmen, Bumble and Dario all fuss around until the camera is actually running, and Elaine has a terrible time trying to keep track of such complicated continuity. The band plays the Sleeping Prince Waltz, while the couples all revolve under the watchful eye of Billy C. Even MM was exhilarated and gave a sparkling performance when she finally arrived. (Music and a new set – both always cheer her up.) We have finished on the gallery and moved to the staircase. The first shot with MM was of her and Jeremy sitting in the middle of it, blocking the paths of the other guests. Lady Sunningdale is stuck behind them and we hear her say, acidly, 'Excuse me, please.' Then we cut to Maxine and see her walk, disapprovingly, round Elsie, and down to the dance floor. It was a good moment to compare the two, one a fading beauty and the other so young and fresh; one so British and one so American. For all the pills and problems, MM looks so full of life and *joie de vivre* in comparison.

The Grand Duke enters the shot from behind and Jeremy persuades them to dance. They went out onto the crowded dance floor, and it was quite a touching scene in a way. MM is a good dancer, and for once SLO's ultra stiff posture made a moving contrast. Our problem was that the extras tend to slow up. They are not as blasé as our regulars, and they all want to be in a close-up shot with SLO and MM. But one can't blame them.

WEDNESDAY, 24 OCTOBER

The good news came at the end of the day. The 'rushes' looked fabulous and even MM, who came to watch for a change, was very impressed. She looked great, the dancers looked great, the set looked great, even SLO looked quite handsome. During the day, things were not so good. For some reason, MM was in a bad temper, so everyone suffered. She was curt with Milton, abrupt with SLO and even snapped at her dresser and her make-up man, which is extremely rare. Plod says that she suspects Milton of some sort of knavery. He also said that she grumbles at AM all the time now.

Even so we managed one very long take in which Elsie and the Grand Duke start to dance. Elsie tries to persuade the Duke to make peace with his son and, as they swirl around, she reads out the young King's conditions. She seemed to forget the last one for a second – genuinely or not I don't know – and then blurted out, 'Oh yes, and he wants a general election.' Strangely enough, it actually worked quite well.

The Grand Duke is dismissive of her attempts to play politics. 'Madame de Pompadour is beyond your range, my dear.' Then he asks 'Do you reverse?' meaning the waltz. MM gave a wild laugh. 'Just try me!' she cried and off they both swept into the crowd.

Only in fairy tales, and films, alas, does such a large crowd dance in such perfect harmony.

But that was all we did get today. The other dancing shots will be done tomorrow, as each requires a new set-up down on the floor. Lots of work for Jack and the stand-ins to do first thing. When MM arrives at her usual hour (8.30), three set-ups a day with her are the best we can hope for. Thank goodness this is such a simple, studio-bound film to shoot.

THURSDAY, 25 OCTOBER

Another day of MM dancing with SLO. The two-shots aren't too bad, but the close-ups are technically very tricky. The cameraman has really to dance with them, and the lighting is critical. In his close-up, SLO had to show that he now realises how delightful this showgirl is, no matter how headstrong and 'disconcerting'. In MM's close-up she had to make it clear that she is now ecstatically in love with the Grand Duke. This was asking quite a lot of both of them. MM was clearly the subject of a technical debate most of the morning, and anyway she was still feeling pretty bad-tempered. Added to that she clearly loathes the man she is meant to be in love with. I think the final – and successful – result was more the result of self-hypnosis than great acting, but perhaps there isn't, or shouldn't be, much difference between the two. In the end we managed four set-ups so we should be out of here by the end of the week.

I had a total surprise when I got back here to Tibbs tonight. Waiting on the doorstep in a hire car were Little David Tennant and Dommy Elwes.* I knew at once that they must be desperate for money, and couldn't but wonder which of them would end up paying the fare! They had found out where I was through Lockhart and Mr Cotes-Preedy at the Club. It turns out that they want me to share a flat with them when the movie is over, and they want to take the flat right now. It is at No 3, Mount Street and has a drawing room overlooking Berkeley Square. It sounded terrific but of course there was a catch. It is quite expensive – £24 per month (£8 each) – and I have to sign the lease, and I have to put up £300 for the privilege (to own the lease). David and Dommy are great fun but they are a couple of rogues. David even insists that he has one of the bathrooms to himself, and Dommy and I share the other one. Dommy has to take what he can get of course. He hasn't got a bean and, I suspect, has no intention of paying the £8 per month either. It seems a bit hard on me but David is so arrogant that one can't argue with him. *He* found the flat, he is doing me a favour etc. Well, I have to live somewhere, and, like all rogues, David and Dommy are very stimulating company. Also it is the only offer I've had, and I hate living alone. So I said 'yes' and duly wrote out a cheque. Dommy is going to start redecorating right away. He is very good at this, but he has very expensive tastes. Right now he tells me he is involved with the two 'geniuses' of interior decoration – a Mr Bonsack and a Mr Fowler.** He says he will make the flat so beautiful that no girl will be able to say 'no' at the crucial moment! I gave him an absolute

* The Hon. David Tennant and Dominic Elwes. Both now dead, alas. (They were both actually quite big – 'Little' was a nickname.)
** Mr Bonsack had a very expensive bathroom shop, and Mr Fowler was the partner in Colefax & Fowler.

spending limit of £400, but limits mean nothing to Dommy. He can charm credit out of a stone. I have lived rent-free for most of the film, and I've spent very little of my wages. Even so it means dipping into GrandPapa's trust – again.

FRIDAY, 26 OCTOBER

We are now at the exit of the ballroom. Elsie is scared of losing her love, but the Grand Duke has his mind firmly set on Lady Sunningdale. The little Ambassador re-appeared for this scene, talking to Lady Sunningdale in the background. I thought he only featured in the coach and the Embassy so I'd forgotten who he was and mistook him for an extra. Luckily I just stopped short of demanding his card when he did not immediately do what he was told. Then MM and SLO did a long scene together – one of the many 'goodbyes' that run through the script. I suspect MM cannot remember which is the last goodbye or which is the important one, so she tends to give them all a lot of heartfelt drama. In today's, Elsie is meant to know that she and Jeremy are only going for a jaunt and that she will soon be back at the Embassy, so they are not saying goodbye for long. But that did not enter into her performance.

'Oh, your Grand Ducal,' she sobbed. 'It's been a great, great ... well ... goodbye.' Luckily one forgets the script where MM is concerned, and it works. 'She's the only one the public will be looking at,' Dame Sybil had said. 'She's really giving everyone else lessons in acting for the cinema.' Nine weeks ago this observation made SLO cross enough. Now it might make a murderer of him, but it is still true.

Talking of Grand Dames, I hear that MM is going to see Dame Edith Sitwell* tomorrow. I could hardly believe it, but

---

* (1887–1964). Poetess, public figure and celebrated English eccentric. She had met MM at a Hollywood tea party in 1952, and invited her to come to tea in London.

Edith is as eccentric as they come and she also adores the limelight. I met Edith with Osbert* at Rennishaw when I was in the RAF. She was hilariously funny and witty and I was in stitches all through lunch. She told how she was on a driving tour of Italy, when they came across a herd of bullocks in the road. 'Drive on' she ordered. Then one bullock stuck its head through her open window, just as the car began to accelerate. 'Stop!' she shrieked, but the driver could not hear, and the bullock had to gallop alongside, its big frightened face an inch from Edith's. Luckily it wasn't a very fast car. I do hope she tells stories like that to MM. It will cheer her up no end.

I didn't say anything of this to MM, or to Milton. Indeed, SLO looked grimly at me as if to say 'Don't you dare.' He knows Edith is a great friend of Mama's, but he clearly conveyed 'Don't get involved, Colin,' and I'm sure he was right. Those two ladies can be as crazy as they like to each other. Neither will understand a word the other is saying, that's for sure, and probably neither will even listen. A highbrow MM is not.

MONDAY, 29 OCTOBER

MM was given the day off today, and quite rightly so. She is going to meet the Queen. First Dame Edith Sitwell and now the Queen! Not bad for a little girl from California. She will be at the first night of *The Battle of the River Plate*** at the Empire Cinema, Leicester Square. Naturally she needed the whole day to get ready for this momentous event and I expect the Queen did too. (They are the same age, actually. The Queen looks a little older, but healthier.) Bumble helped MM to choose a suitable dress and was at Parkside all day overseeing

---

* Edith's younger brother (1892–1969). Poet, novelist, biographer, autobiographer. Rennishaw Hall was the Sitwell family home in Derbyshire.
** Directed by Michael Powell and Emeric Pressburger. It was released in the US under the title *Pursuit of the Graf Spee*. Tony Bushell was one of the principal actors.

preparations. Bumble is actually a very calming person. She always seems to be so wrapped up in her own nervous twitches that she doesn't have time to take any notice of yours. The effect is very endearing and MM likes her. Plod is very thrilled about the whole affair. His protégée, as he thinks of MM, is going to meet his monarch. Of course he will be there in the car, protecting MM just as his friends protect H.M. If Plod is excited, MM is in a complete spin. Plod said she has been curtseying all over the house and even trying to talk in an English accent, goodness knows why. I suppose that meeting the Queen is a wonderful sign of success for every actor and actress. Even MM can't ignore that, and any encouragement is so good for her soul that I am happy for her. More than anything, MM wants to feel accepted, and to her the invitation to a great Premiere like this, and shaking hands with Royalty, means that she has been accepted as one of the great actresses of her time. She is no longer just a sex symbol or a calendar girl. She is making a film with Sir Laurence Olivier. The Queen is not to know that the film is on the verge of falling apart because MM is always late and cannot remember her lines. Indeed, I'm sure that the Queen wouldn't care two pins even if someone had told her. Film-making is as much a mystery to H.M. as it is to most people. It is only the finished movie that matters. All actresses throw tantrums and have done since time began. If the Queen did but know, MM throws fewer than most. Only someone very unkind would suggest that it is the Queen's advisers who choose the latest Hollywood freak to amuse their mistress. Certainly not me.

TUESDAY, 30 OCTOBER

MM got rave reviews for her appearance last night. 'MM Captures Britain' was one headline. But in Studio A the drama continues. I suppose MM stayed up very late and so was extra tired today. The trouble is that she takes extra pills when she doesn't feel 100%, without really knowing what effect the pills will have. If I take a pill and it makes me feel lousy, I don't take it again. Not MM. She just takes another pill to counteract the first one. As a result she was at her most distant and remote. When she is like that, no one can talk to her. It just isn't worth the effort. This is so sad, because she should be on top of the world. Drugs just spoil everything. I know how tempting they are and goodness knows I can't preach. I take too much alcohol, and too many cigarettes. MM looks more and more vulnerable and I am sorry for her. But when a whole studio is waiting to do an expensive and complicated shot, going ga-ga is not the way to be popular.

This morning, during one of the inevitable long delays, I went up into the lighting grid. I was invited, I hasten to add. You never *dare* to stray into anyone else's little kingdom here without being invited, especially the Kingdom of the Sparks. It is incredibly hot. All the heat of the studio lights is trapped up there. The extractor fans are turned off during filming, and then the place is airtight. There are far more men up there than I realised, mostly in string vests. I never thought they took any notice of what went on below them on the studio floor, but they know everything and everybody. They cannot stand MM. Even *they* get frustrated, waiting around for her to start work, and to remember a single line. They are real old pros, veterans of countless Rank films, and they think of MM as totally unprofessional. I tried to explain that it wasn't fair to expect MM to be like Norman Wisdom,* but they weren't having it. 'If it wasn't for our loyalty to Sir Laurence,' said one, seriously, 'I'd have edged a spanner off the grid and onto her head.' I'm very glad indeed they haven't gone that far.

When I went into SLO's dressing room with the whisky and

---

* Durable British comic actor, b.1918.

cigs this evening he was alone. Tony goes back to London now and Milton had dashed home with MM. SLO wanted to chat and even offered me a drink.

'Can you believe it Colin? Am I doing such a bad job? Anyway it doesn't matter.' The poor man slumped in his make-up chair, wiping his face. 'The bloody Strasbergs have won the day with Milton, and Paula will be back tomorrow.'

'Maybe that will put MM in a better humour,' I suggested.

'I have never been in a situation like this before, Colin and you can be bloody sure I never will again. It's a f—ing nightmare. I thought this would be an exciting challenge, a renaissance, I thought Marilyn would make me feel young again. Some bloody hope. I feel dead. I look dead in the bloody rushes. It's killing me.'

'It won't be long now, Sir Laurence,' I said. 'We must keep our nerve.' He grunted.

I can see he feels completely smothered. If only he'd stuck to acting. He thought his role as Grand Duke was so easy, especially after the theatre, that he might as well direct too, and of course get the extra money. Little did he know what went on beneath MM's famous bosom!

WEDNESDAY, 31 OCTOBER

SLO was late. He even arrived after MM for once. ('F— her' he said when I told him.) But he was still on the set long before MM. He is so professional that he can easily get made up and dressed in half an hour if he wants to, just as he does in the theatre.

MM's retreat into a fantasy world is getting more common every day. It is both the cause of, and is caused by, MM's growing unpopularity. If any of us talk to her she looks at them as if they belonged to a different species, and this does make it very hard to like her. Even the most kind-hearted members of the crew, who understand some of MM's problems – and I like to think this includes me – still get frustrated and fed up.

The Digs scene we shot today should be a very nice one. Dicky W is sitting behind a screen – all elegant legs and blasé voice – while Elsie dashes round, choosing a dress. She is helped by her roommate, the divine Daphne Anderson. It is at the beginning of the story, and Elsie clearly thinks that she is invited to a big Embassy reception, even though she can't think why. Daphne – who does know why, or at least can guess – clucks round with sisterly concern. Elsie didn't seem to need any special 'motivation' except the obvious one of a girl trying to get the right dress on. But soon MM was dashing backwards and forwards to her recliner, shaking her hands like a dervish, even though you can't imagine two more sympathetic professionals to act with than Dicky and Daphne.

THURSDAY, 1 NOVEMBER

Winter is almost here, but the film seems to go on and on. Are all films such agony? Those balmy summer days with my little Wdg seem literally years ago. But showbiz has its compensations. Tonight Milton had a wonderful dinner party. It is already 11.30 but I must make a note of it before I go to sleep.

The main guest was Gene Kelly, and he is quite incredible – friendly, positive, unassuming and fantastically witty. He can mimic anyone, dance on a sixpence, sing like an angel and tell endless jokes. At one stage I remarked to him how much I had enjoyed the Bolshoi Ballet* – I was trying to impress him I suppose, since only a few people have been able to get anywhere near Bolshoi performances. He immediately jumped up and did an impression of Ulanova which was devastating – but also touching. After all she is about 45 and still dancing Giselle, albeit magically well. Gene Kelly managed to convey all this as he danced in the dining room of Tibbs Farm, humming his own rendition of the music. Most impressive, and there is no doubt what got him to the top – talent. The other star guest was a glamorous star*let*. She is an Italian girl called Elsa Martinelli** and she has had a special place in my affections ever since I was 15. I had a colour photograph of her pinned up inside my 'bury'*** at Eton. In it she had on very short jeans and a revealing wet shirt. Attired thus, she alternately drove me crazy and stimulated me to action for two years. I suppose

---

* The Bolshoi Ballet was visiting London for the first time since the war. My father had a box for the opening night as he was on the Board of the Royal Opera House. I had taken a beautiful young actress called Maureen Swanson (now Countess of Dudley) but it had been a total failure, which is why I didn't mention it in my diary.

** b.1933. Her English-language films included *Manuela*, *The Trial*, *Marco the Magnificent*.

*** Eton slang for desk ('bureau').

the 'real thing' could never quite match a posed pin-up. Miss Martinelli is still beautiful, but eight years older now of course. She is also very unpleasant. She is gratuitously nasty; she rarely smiles, and she loves to put people down (especially me), so that's the end of that love affair! I'm certainly glad we aren't making *The Sleeping Prince* with *her* playing Elsie Marina.

Even so, Milton is a wonderful host, and David Maysles is an excellent foil, so the whole thing went really well. It was almost impossible for me to get up and leave the room. GK and EM are staying the night. EM has a near perfect figure – or at least she had in that picture. Even so I didn't want to sleep with her. Poison is poison, no matter which bottle it's in.

FRIDAY, 2 NOVEMBER

Usually Milton controls his energy much better than I do. That is possibly why he is so successful. But today he looked very grey. Alas it looks as if he has finally fallen out with SLO. He – Milton – is fed up with being responsible for delivering MM to the studio every morning, and taking her bad temper all day. 'I'm not her nanny,' he said plaintively this evening. 'Olivier should scream at Paula. She has more influence than me. Tell him to scream at Arthur, Colin. See if that helps.'

We all know that it is no good screaming at any of them. SLO is getting very frustrated. After all Milton *did* promise to get MM to the studio for work. He did assure SLO that he was in control. He did promise to restrict Paula to MM's dressing room and so on and so on. Milton is the only person SLO can scream at (except for Tony and me), and when SLO has to scream, he screams.

And Tony is being really short with Milton, which is a sure sign that SLO is being very rude about Milton behind his back. Tony would never dare to do that off his own bat. If filming goes according to plan – the new Mk III plan, that is, not the original Perceval cross-plot – then we will be finished shooting in two weeks. Surely we can last till then.

We were in the Elsie's dressing-room set today, and MM was being very erratic. She grabbed a huge powder puff and covered herself in powder, and then she re-arranged her hair in the mirror. This sort of behaviour is fine in a real music-hall dressing room, but on a film set it gives hysterics to make-up, wardrobe, wigs, continuity (Elaine), camera (Denys) and sound (Mitch). I suppose it did make a bit of a mess but the effect was like that of a hand grenade.

We had just finished a scene with old Gladys Henson as the dresser. She and MM had both got so nervous that we nearly gave up and went home. 'My shoulder thing is busted' was the best we could get for the essential reference to a pinned strap which will break again in front of the Grand Duke. We are saved by the fact that all the other actresses are absolute stalwarts, who never panic, no matter what. Take after take they produce the same flawless performances, as if it was the first. I suppose if they were all nervous Americans they could all have hysterics together, and get it over and done with. A sort of camaraderie might have grown up which would embrace MM instead of excluding her. These people would love to include MM, but they just do not speak the same language. The result is that she feels, and becomes, more and more remote. We all feel helpless and frustrated.

I must get some sleep. Stars can afford nervous breakdowns, senior crew are allowed to have a headache, 3rd Ast Dirs must stay in rude health. No energy, no job.

MONDAY, 5 NOVEMBER

Guy Fawkes night, and no prizes for guessing where we would like to plant a bomb. But she didn't turn up at all this morning, so we had a relatively peaceful day.

Milton is not quite so quick to go to SLO's dressing room after rushes these days, nor quite so welcome, and Tony heads off for London. This means that I can usually stay for a chat and a drink. SLO likes to unwind with big whiskies and Olivier cigarettes for half an hour before going home to Vivien. Tonight the poor man was already worrying about what he will do next. He has to continue working on the film – editing, adding music, special effects etc. until after Christmas – but then he wants to find a new challenge. He is obsessed with the fact that he will be 50 next year, and sees this as a big turning point. Famous as he is, he is not interested in the successes of the past. He feels he has a far greater contribution still to make, and is not prepared to rest on his laurels. All the trappings of being a star he sees as hindrances – Notley, the knighthood, even, to some extent, Vivien. It is wonderful to be so ambitious – at 50! He very kindly said that he hopes I will stay with him, whatever he does. Of course he cannot guarantee anything. He may accept a job working for somebody else. That would probably be a relief to start with, although he is too experienced to be told what to do except by a very few, brilliant directors.

'But you are part of the family now, Colin,' he said, and that is what I wanted to hear more than anything else. Loyalty is what he demands and then he is fiercely loyal back. He certainly won't go straight into another film – he couldn't stand it – so that means the theatre. But which play? And for whom?* Right

---

* In fact his next project was to be one of the most unexpected and significant stage performances of his career – as Archie Rice in John Osborne's *The Entertainer* at the Royal Court, directed by George Devine.

now he has to get this film finished somehow. It's much too late for him to find a new approach – to MM or to anyone else in her group. He does realise that Milton is trying his best, but he has lost some of his respect for him. He knows that AM is only too keen to get MM out of the house in the mornings, and for this reason alone is an ally. He can see that everyone else in the film is rooting for him, and giving all the help they can. But still: 'Frankly Colin, I've had it' is his constant refrain. 'Vivien is being very difficult. She is clearly fed up with the whole thing. She never liked the idea – hated it in fact. She was jealous, I suppose, although she'd never admit that.' Now she is bored. Doesn't want to listen to SLO's moans any more. She always hated early nights. She won't respect film discipline. She's started the old round of house guests and dinner parties and late nights at Notley. 'I don't like that, Colin. In fact I hate it.'

(I haven't bothered to put in all the swear words, but there were plenty.) The truth is that, once again, Vivien doesn't let him get enough sleep. Fancy being tormented by both these women at once – Vivien Leigh and Marilyn Monroe. And I get the impression that he isn't having sex with either!

TUESDAY, 6 NOVEMBER

We are still in Elsie's dressing room at the theatre. The 'girls', Elsie's companions, with minor roles to play, are what keep us all going. They are completely unspoilt, and are thrilled to be working with MM, which makes them a joy. MM is so famous that any actress could be forgiven for thinking that a little of that fame must rub off. Vera Day plays, and is, a cheeky Cockney. Her husband came to collect her this evening and we met in the long corridor. I soon found out why she bothered to introduce him to me. 'I wonder if you could do me a favour Colin,' he said immediately. I murmured that I'd be delighted to try. 'Right then. Go to the editing room and get a few frames of film with Vera in the picture with Marilyn. I'll see you all right,' he added, and pressed a 2 shilling piece into my hand. 'There's another of those for you when you get the film.' That was more naive than I thought.

'No, no, that's frightfully kind of you,' I said, 'but I can't take it. I'll certainly try to find the film, but Sir Laurence would never allow me to accept a reward. Thank you so much for such a generous offer.' He looks like an Old Kent Road bruiser, and he wasn't too pleased to have his 'generous' tip returned. I wonder what I would have done if he'd offered me a 'fiver'? Actually it won't be too easy to do what he asks. I'll have to ask the ast editor for a trim. He will only let me have something shot before the clapper or after the cut and I don't think Vera is in shot with MM very often, except in the middle of a scene.

WEDNESDAY, 7 NOVEMBER

A new film has started shooting at Pinewood with Bob Hope and Katharine Hepburn. It is a comedy called *The Iron Petticoat*. Everyone was dying to meet Hope and dreaded working with Hepburn. Needless to say Hepburn is *divine* and BH is arrogant and unpleasant.

Hepburn says hello to everyone while Hope remains totally aloof. I met Hepburn today when she came to visit SLO. She is as gorgeous as Dame Sybil, only much younger, all red hair, and freckles, and a huge smile which she turned on me as often as on SLO. SLO did have a point when he said later: 'Why couldn't MM have been like that? What a lot of fun we could have had, making this film.'*

* Katharine Hepburn had been a witness at SLO's secret marriage to Vivien in California in 1940. In 1973 she and SLO made their only acting appearance together, as the ageing couple in *Love Among the Ruins*, directed by George Cukor for American television.

'Yes, but MM's had twice the publicity and half the training as an actress. That would derange anyone.'

'No training as an actress at all,' said SLO gloomily. And yet he is forgetting what Dame Sybil said about who the public will be looking at when the film comes out.

My main goal now is to keep SLO cheerful. But I have a dilemma. Do I stick to SLO when all this is over, and hope that he will take me to the theatre with him? Or do I stick to David, and the film gang, and try to get a job as a 2nd Ast Dir with them on their next movie? I haven't talked it over with David yet and that is going to be hard to do without seeming to presume that he would help me.

David can be very touchy and he has always been ambivalent about having a 3rd Ast Dir with 'connections'. I'd really have to dump those 'connections' completely to stay with him. The film world is '*sauve qui peut*'. It is dangerous to presume too much, even though David and Mr P are two people I really feel I can trust to help.

THURSDAY, 8 NOVEMBER

We are now back-stage at the Gaiety Theatre. The Grand Duke is making his visit to the cast in the interval, and they will all be lined up to be introduced. In the rushes of yesterday's footage, MM looked really embarrassing, as if she came from a different production altogether – the mad woman of Chaillott.* Her hair was down and her eyes were wild. Her line 'Oh gosh! I don't have a thing to wear' came out like the cry of a drowning woman – and, come to think about it, that's really what it was!

Today she was more cheerful. She was among a whole group of actors and actresses who treated her pretty much as one of them – a bunch of players thrown together in minor roles in

* Play by Jean Giraudoux (1882–1944). It was filmed in 1969 starring, coincidentally, Katharine Hepburn.

a musical comedy. As they all jostled round, pushing and chattering, she must have felt like she did in the Actors' Studio, But tonight MM complained to Paula that she was feeling ill. Paula can no longer speak to anyone English but me, so I act as interpreter. I rushed the news to David first this time, so he could warn Jack and the crew. An early warning like this definitely means that she will not be in tomorrow. Then I went to SLO's dressing room to break it to him gently over a whisky.

'Quick. Warn the crew before they go home.'

'Done.'

'Well try to find Milton, and see if she'll see a doctor. She might be off for five days.'

'Milton's already gone to Parkside to see what he can arrange.'

'Oh. Good,' SLO said doubtfully. He likes me to think for him, but I suppose sometimes it makes him feel old.

'I'm afraid MM is a very healthy young woman,' I said. 'She's just in bad condition. No regular meals, sleep or exercise. Pills one day, champagne the next. No wonder she feels ill but I don't think she *is* ill.'

SLO growled. 'Discipline is the most important thing for an actor. An actor can be permanently drunk, like Bob Newton or Charles Laughton, so long as they have discipline. Without it any actor just falls apart.'

'MM is too spoiled now,' I said. As long as everyone keeps telling her she is a genius and can do no wrong, she won't understand why she should go to sleep, or eat, or turn up at the same time as normal people. It's no good saying 'Marilyn, you are a normal person underneath.' She is completely convinced that her extraordinary fame exempts her completely. What no one dares to tell her is that her fame springs mainly – but not entirely – from her appearance.

'You know, I actually fancied her when I first met her,' said SLO. 'She's a freak of nature, not a genius. A beautiful freak.'

FRIDAY, 9 NOVEMBER

Since we knew MM wasn't coming in, we were all prepared. Everyone is sympathetic to SLO, and tries to help if they can. He looks pretty gloomy all the time, and his performance gets less and less appealing. This is a special pity because what we are shooting now is his first appearance in the film, apart from his arrival in the coach.

MM's first appearance was the mad scene with the powder puff, so they are a pretty sorry pair. (I wonder if that is why she was so nervous then. I hadn't thought of that – but maybe, just maybe, she had.)

Tony B is not as friendly to me these days. That's sad, after all the happy times we had together at Runnymede. I hope it doesn't reflect something that SLO has said to him. Actually I think it is because he is slightly jealous. He is so very possessive of 'Laurence', as he calls him sternly. But he is still a lovely man, and mellows quite quickly when I pretend I haven't noticed him being cool. I don't know if he also expects to move on with SLO. Perhaps SLO has told Vivien – just to please her – that he is taking me with him into the theatre. Vivien's world is built on 'Chums' or – in my case, as with Gilman – adoring slaves. Tony is a SLO man, not a Vivien man. He likes to go off with SLO while Anne stays with Vivien. Now the film is ending, Vivien's influence is growing stronger every day. We will know in 10 days' time.

SATURDAY, 10 NOVEMBER

This morning I just couldn't resist doing a practical joke on Milton and David. The phone rang when we were all having drinks at lunchtime. I was sitting beside it so I picked it up.

'Does Mr Greene need a car over the weekend?' asked a

voice. 'Now, listen here Marilyn,' I said crisply. 'I've had enough of your bad behaviour. You're late, you're rude and you don't learn your lines . . .'

By this time Milton and David M had both reached the phone, arms and legs flailing wildly.

'Marilyn, Marilyn, we love you!' they screamed at the startled hire car company. 'Don't listen to him. It was Colin. He's gone crazy. We love you!' I was laughing so much that they began to smell a rat. 'Marilyn? Marilyn?'

'Is that the Greene residence?' said the chauffeur at the end of the line.

I don't know if they will forgive me. I suppose it was cruel of me after so much hospitality. They pretend to see the funny side, but Milton was badly shaken. Even David M 'lost his cool' for a minute or two. At dinner tonight Milton looked at me strangely.

'I didn't know you Brits had it in you,' he said, whatever that means.

MONDAY, 12 NOVEMBER

Seven more days, and then we will all have to go back to the real world. For 15 weeks we have been hermetically sealed in a huge concrete box, like animals in a zoo. We are almost completely cut off from life outside. We arrive in the dark before anyone else is awake and leave in the dark after they are back home again. The average is 13 hours a day. Somehow we have all managed to get along, except, I suppose, for poor MM (and the little Wdg). No one can approach MM now. If you address her directly, you might as well talk in Swahili. She is, no doubt, more desperate to get out than we are. That, however, was not 'motivation' enough to get her to the studio today. Plod rang early – 'Not a chance.' SLO was in a towering rage. The whole cast of *The Coconut Girl* had been called, and there was only one scene we could shoot with them. This consisted of Jean Kent – the leading lady – lining up everyone back-stage ready for the Grand Duke's arrival. As she is finishing she has to ask 'Now. Who's missing?'

'Elsie Marina,' calls Daphne.

'Oh, can't that girl *ever* make an entrance on time?' Miss Springfield replies, crossly. The irony was lost on nobody.

After lunch we did the part of the Grand Duke's progress down the line where he meets Vera Day. Up until now the film has only had one female in it – namely MM, if you don't count old Dame S. I think SLO sometimes forgets what real girls are like. Little Vera Day gave off more energy than SLO expected. He seemed taken aback and almost forgot his lines for a moment – unheard of for SLO. Of course he is very tense, and perhaps he is so brainwashed by MM and Vivien that he expects all women to be difficult. Vera is simple, direct, and sexy. She radiates a different sort of life force to MM. It is lower voltage – and not so far reaching – but it is strong enough to give you a jolt. SLO is normally so wooden, Dicky so dry and Jeremy so discreet that it is little wonder that MM jumps out of the screen every night in 'rushes'. She really has had no competition at all. No one could deny MM's natural talents, and I'm not suggesting that Vera Day could carry the movie, but even so, SLO got a surprise. It was like a man who works in a power station getting an electric shock from his car battery.

I have certainly missed female company over the last 15 weeks. I suppose it's not until you get to be a producer that you sleep with the starlets. I hope there are more opportunities in the theatre. If not, I have a dangerous tendency to fall in love with other people's wives.

TUESDAY, 13 NOVEMBER

At last we have done MM's entrance into the line-up. As the Grand Duke enters through the fire doors and walks onto the stage, Elsie Marina can be seen joining the line in the background. She is in full stage make-up with a feathered hat. MM had bolted in from her recliner next to her portable dressing room in such a hectic flurry that most of the cast, who were agog to see this incredible creature at last, were disappointed. Then the whole apparition vanished again just as quickly when Tony said 'Cut.' Up until now, the timing of her performance has been set throughout the film by her, and this is by design. SLO saw that was something that you could not alter. Today's entrance required split-second precision of the kind she absolutely hates. There were many false attempts and too many people trying to 'cue her in'. We only just had time to do the two-shot where Daphne tries to calm her down – on screen and in real life. MM looked over-excited to meet the Regent. It was as if Elsie was already wondering if he would be attractive and whether she could seduce him, and this is not the way the plot works. But SLO could not throttle her back. Perhaps she is happier hiding behind the heavy 'stage' make-up; perhaps she feels that the end is nigh; or perhaps she had had an extra glass of champagne. (It is not that MM drinks too much, but sometimes at unwise times.)

WEDNESDAY, 14 NOVEMBER

One last big scene with MM. The Grand Duke is coming down the line. MM is in the foreground. She is panicky.
'What do I do?'
Daphne consoles her. 'Just say "How do you do?" ' etc.
The manager of the theatre says 'Miss Elsie Marina.'

Grand Duke: 'And the little American friend of our heroine. How do you do?'

By this time MM is desperately trying not to anticipate what is about to happen. 'How do you do, your Regent,' she says. 'Oops,' and her shoulder strap breaks. As she nearly popped out of the low-cut dress, she instinctively turned from the camera, as if from a prying eye, but it worked well.

'The damage, I trust, can be retrieved,' says a delighted Grand Duke.

Elsie, panting for breath: 'Oh yes, I can fix it with a pin.'

The GD looks round. 'Has no one here a pin?' All the men feel their lapels, where flower girls have pinned carnations on them in the past.

GD: 'I would be most happy to assist you.'

Elsie, still confused (and MM even more confused!): 'No, your Regency.'

Pause while she scrabbles to fix the dress.

GD: 'Charming.' He goes to shake hands. 'Better not tempt Providence again.' Laughs. 'Charming. Good night!' He exits.

Actually it is the same stunt that MM pulled at her original press conference with SLO in the USA and one that I expect she has often used to get attention. The hard part was to include it in a pre-rehearsed scene for the camera. But it's all done now, and at one stage that was more than we dared hope. Of course this isn't the end of the job, for us or for MM. She doesn't fly home for a week. We have two days of 'post-syncing' in which MM will re-do her voice for the sound track. She must record any lines which were said off camera, and re-record sentences where her voice wasn't picked up clearly enough. (There hadn't been anywhere suitable to put a microphone when she was face down on the sofa etc.) But at least this means that she doesn't need to be in until 9 a.m. – which she hasn't been for a couple of weeks anyway – and she doesn't need make-up and wardrobe before work. Having said this, Monday and Tuesday have been set aside for possible 'pick up' shots, and for those she will need to be dolled up exactly as before. Elaine will see to that. Jack Harris and his assistant are frantically assembling a 'rough cut' to see which shots need covering. There is no question that we might have missed a shot by mistake, but it is extremely hard, over all these weeks, to make a seamless pattern and overlook nothing. So they will work tomorrow and Friday and all weekend. One thing is for sure – once MM has caught that plane back to the USA, that is it. No chance for one more frame of film of her, no matter how great the crisis.

So there were no celebrations. Milton says that he has arranged a party for Tuesday afternoon, after the last retake. But actually David Maysles tells me that he has been left to organise it. And quite frankly he couldn't care less.

FRIDAY, 16 NOVEMBER

It was as if a great weight had been lifted off everyone's shoulders. SLO was looking relaxed and years younger. MM was cool and efficient. She never looks at SLO these days, or talks to anyone, but she listened intently to the sound editor's instructions and obeyed them to the letter. As a result she got through far more than we could have imagined, and, I must say, did it extremely well. Post-syncing is a knack, like formation-flying or dancing the tango. MM picked it up immediately, and even seemed to enjoy it. Her face and her voice would appear on the screen and she would watch intently, two or three times. Then she would wave her hand and her face would appear without the voice. She put her words in so exactly that we couldn't tell, in the director's booth, that it wasn't pre-recorded. The song was the same. MM always enjoys music scenes and in the end we were all rather moved by this quiet, shy, firm voice. Just for once, MM could go back to Parkside feeling good about herself, but I don't think that is the memory which will endure.

This evening we had a long post-mortem. I was surprised by how much the Americans resented us. I have to admit that I had always assumed that we were the charming well-behaved ones, and the Americans were the trouble makers. Of course they see things quite the other way. They think we are cold, unwelcoming and clique-y. 'Not you, Colin,' Milton put in, with a laugh, 'or we wouldn't have let you in the house.' By and large, we have been as disappointing as hosts as they – well, some of them – have been as guests. In the end I felt sad and apologetic. We haven't exactly behaved badly, but we have been very blinkered to other people's needs – to Milton's, to Paula's, to Arthur's and especially to MM's. It's not as if they had all been monsters in the Arthur P. Jacobs mould. Stupidly, I had assumed that we all had the same aim – to make a good film, on time and on budget. I see now that life is never as simple as that. Everyone, me included, has many other reasons for doing what they did. I really want to start a career, to make a good personal impression even if the film is a flop. I want to persuade SLO that he can't do without me and that he must take me into the theatre with him. MM wanted to change the direction of her career, to be taken seriously in a 'classical' acting role, with a great 'classical' actor. She couldn't expect to play Lady Macbeth straight away, but she wanted something that she could handle without relying solely on her sex appeal. For Milton, it was his first motion picture, his chance to prove to Warner Bros that he could deliver a film as executive producer. It was also a chance to make money. Being a photographer clearly hadn't made him as rich as he'd like.

What a pity that they didn't all sit down and work out what

they wanted before the filming started. But then everything was excitement and optimism, and publicity. Serious thought was not encouraged. I understand why Mr Perceval was so grave, but he was the only one. SLO could claim that he'd scheduled rehearsals to be as well prepared as possible, but he and MM were both so on edge that a genuine dialogue was always unlikely. They should have had a quick affair together, and got onto each other's wavelength, at least. There certainly isn't going to be a 'next time'. All that we can hope now is that we've produced a good film. At the moment it is impossible to tell.

MONDAY, 19 NOVEMBER

Surely this was the hardest day of all. After lengthy conferences on Sunday between Jack (editor) and Jack (cameraman), Milton, SLO and Tony, they decided to do two more shots of MM, one more shot with SLO, and, if possible, one shot of both of them together. We started with MM. Make-up, Hair and Wardrobe had all been called for a normal studio day. In a way they were pleased. It is so hard to change the habits you have acquired over 100 days of doing the same thing – we were like patients in a mental hospital when the front door has been left open. Carmen and Roger and Dario had been running round to find the right pieces of set. Jack had to match up the lighting, Elaine was at her strictest, scouring her notes and peering at frames of 35mm film through a magnifying glass. I wonder if anyone explained to MM that these shots are not to correct failures on her part, but to fill in gaps other people may have left. I doubt it, by her behaviour, but then it is pretty hard to explain anything by now. She turned up later than ever, fretted terribly and retreated again and again into her dressing room. All Jack (Harris) really needed were two shots of MM for insurance – one in her white dress against an out-of-focus purple room; and one in her dress and frilly coat in an equally out-of-focus hall. There is a piece of purple wall still existing (thanks to the foresight of Teddy Joseph), and many bits of hall, so that was all right. But MM behaved like a drugged prisoner of war. We did get both shots but goodness knows if they are remotely usable. I suppose they might be better than nothing. We will watch them in rushes tomorrow – in the morning for a change so – theoretically – SLO can ask MM to do them again if necessary. We also filmed SLO going to a window in the purple room, and looking back at camera. None of this seemed to harmonise too well with the original stuff, at least to my eye. It will depend on the skill of the two Jacks.

When MM left the studio, she did so quickly and furtively. She is supposed to come back tomorrow but we all know she won't. She didn't say goodbye to anyone, not even her personal dresser, who has been so loyal and patient, or to Gordon, her hairdresser.

We knew we would never see her again and, sad to tell, it was an immense relief. Poor Milton is very depressed. He feels a failure, but he would have needed the strength of ten men to have succeeded in all his roles. He had been warned about what he was taking on by other producers of MM's films. But her appeal is so great that he shrugged them off. Even MM is not to blame. The great engine of publicity that surrounds her is unstoppable. Like some awful curse of the gods, it stalks her every moment, and one day it will crush her.

TUESDAY, 20 NOVEMBER

Back at Pinewood for the last time.

Another shot of SLO, this time with the camera looking up at him from the floor – the point of view MM would have had when she slid to the ground after too much vodka. No one can find the ceiling piece, painted with cherubs, to which MM refers, so we had to go without it. SLO was stony-faced. He is not a happy man at the moment.

By lunchtime it was crystal clear that we wouldn't see MM again.

Mr Perceval came in to supervise the winding down of the production. He has asked me to help him clear up in the London office for another 10 days, but he still has Vanessa, so he is just being kind. Then the production office will be closed and LOP will vanish, I suppose. SLO explained that he will start editing next week. To my great relief, he did make a definite date for me to come to see him in London at the end of January. 'Don't worry, Colin. We won't let you starve. We'll find something for you to do.'

This is just as well as I got no encouragement from David at all. He sees me as part of SLO's team now – about to disappear with the rest of them. After lunch we did a shot of Dicky Wattis's stand-in's legs behind a screen – supposed to be in Elsie Marina's digs, while Dicky is waiting for her to get ready to go to the Embassy. MM had had a struggle to get into that tight white dress at the best of times. On camera, and helped only by Daphne, it had proved impossible. We desperately needed the 'cut-away' to cover Bumble and the dresser going in to help sort it out. It was very sad not to see Dicky himself. He and Paul became great friends and I will miss them.

After the last shot was over, there was a great sense of let-down. Milton and David Maysles appeared and invited us all into the next studio, which is not in use. At one end there was a large trestle table covered with packages.

'Men on the left, women on the right,' they called. 'A parting gift to each one of you – from Marilyn.'

Everyone pressed forward to look. At the men's end the packages were obviously bottles – identically wrapped. At the other end were smaller objects which turned out to be identical leather purses. Each item had been labelled with the name of someone on the crew. People rummaged around, finding the present with their name on. Then one man, I didn't see who, walked across the studio to one of the huge round rubbish bins. He stood there for a moment, and then he just threw his bottle in. Immediately one of the ladies followed and threw in her purse. There was a sort of rippling murmur of anger and assent, and then everyone followed suit. Quite soon the bin was literally overflowing with bottles and purses, still wrapped and labelled – 'Thank you from Marilyn Monroe' in David's handwriting. For Milton that was too much; he shrugged and grinned and left. I had already said my goodbyes as I loaded up the car this morning. I expect we will all recover. But it's going to take a long time.

POSTSCRIPT

We never saw Marilyn again, but we knew exactly what was going to happen. She would fall out completely with Milton Greene (she did, in 1957), and Marilyn Monroe Productions would never make another film (it didn't). Her marriage to Arthur Miller would collapse and end in divorce (it did, in 1961). She would become unable to work at all, and would eventually commit suicide (she did, in 1962). Had we been told about conspiracy theories and Kennedy connections, we would simply have shrugged our shoulders. The pressure of just being Marilyn Monroe was already making each day a painful struggle for her, and the end of the story was inevitable.

While she was making *The Prince and the Showgirl*, Marilyn was often in great distress. Of course she was in an unfamiliar foreign country, but even those with whom she had chosen to surround herself were from a completely different world to her. Milton and Amy Greene, Lee and Paula Strasberg, Arthur Miller, Hedda Rosten, Arthur Jacobs and Irving Stein all came from a New York, Jewish, immigrant background which was the opposite of Marilyn's unstructured Californian upbringing. Not for her the possessive mother in the warm Bronx kitchen, giving a child a sense of its own worth, and the future confidence that goes with it. And yet, when she was in front of a camera, Marilyn radiated a joy and a vitality which made everyone else pale by comparison. No wonder we cannot forget her.

It was clear that *The Prince and the Showgirl* was not destined to be a big success at the box office. It was too 'stagy' and too claustrophobic. Nor would the film make much impact on the career of either of its two stars. Paradoxically, it was Olivier's performance that was most affected by the problems on the set. Despite his unprintable comments about her inexperience and unprofessionalism, Marilyn had appeared in virtually the same number of films as he had (*The Prince and the Showgirl* was her twenty-fifth to his twenty-eighth), and her relationship with the camera was more intimate than his – Dame Sybil was right. Watching the film today, Marilyn appears happy and natural, while Olivier often looks stiff and awkward.

Marilyn's next film role, in *Some Like it Hot*, brought her great critical acclaim, but no relief from the problems of production. Many years after it was made I met the director, Billy Wilder, at a Hollywood party. Stuck for something to say to this fierce old Austrian, I murmured that I too had worked with Miss Monroe. 'Then you know the meaning of pure pain,' he growled, and stalked away. Yes – but of pure magic too.

Laurence Olivier did not forget his promise to take me with him. He had found a play which would give him the new lease of life he had been looking for. *The Entertainer* by John Osborne opened at the Royal Court Theatre on 10 April 1957, and is still considered one of Olivier's greatest performances. I became his personal assistant, and also the Assistant Stage Manager at the Court. We took the play on tour and then to the Palace Theatre in the West End. Halfway through the run Joan Plowright took over the role created by Dorothy Tutin, and Olivier's marriage to Vivien Leigh finally collapsed. By this time I had accompanied Larry and Vivien on the Royal Shakespeare Theatre's tour of Europe with *Titus Andronicus*, but that is the subject of a different diary.

I never worked on another feature film, and in the film world you are either in or out. Consequently I never saw David Orton or Mr Perceval again; but I owe them both a debt of gratitude. I continued my friendship with Tony and Anne Bushell, and I often visited Larry in his dressing-room wherever he happened to be performing. Vivien I saw up until the last week of her life in July 1967.

After Olivier went to Hollywood to make *Spartacus* in 1959 I was offered a job by Sidney Bernstein, Chairman of Granada Television. Once more I had high hopes, but I soon found myself back where I had started, as a trainee Assistant Floor Manager. Eventually I did become a producer and director – of documentary films on 'the Arts', of which I made over a hundred. It has been a rewarding and enjoyable career, and I never forgot the lessons I learned on *The Prince and the Showgirl.*

INDEX